SuperBikes
FROM AROUND THE WORLD

SuperBikes
FROM AROUND THE WORLD

REVISED AND UPDATED BY ROLAND BROWN
With contributions by
Mac McDiarmid, Tom Isitt and Kevin Raymond

Page 1 – Ducati's ST2 Sport Turismo combines the Italian firm's traditional high performance and V-twin character with the comfort required of a top-class all-rounder.

Page 2 – The stylish and super-fast ZX-7R, Kawasaki's best 750cc super-sports bike yet, is the end product of many years of development by the Japanese firm.

Page 3 – Honda's ultra-light CBR900RR Fireblade stunned the motorcycle world when it was released, and has since been refined to keep it at the front of the sports-bike pack.

This is a Parragon Book

© Parragon 1997
Reprinted in 1998

Parragon
13 Whiteladies Road, Clifton,
Bristol BS8 1PB, United Kingdom

Designed and produced by
Stonecastle Graphics Limited
Old Chapel Studio, Plain Road, Marden,
Tonbridge, Kent TN12 9LS, United Kingdom

ISBN 0-75252-666-9

Printed in Italy

Photographic credits

Roland Brown: pages 1, 15 (top), 16, 18, 34, 35 (top), 49 (below), 74
Paul Bryant: page 49 (top)
Jason Critchell: pages 90, 91 (top)
Gold & Goose: pages 2, 3, 38, 39, 48, 54, 56, 57, 72, 73, 75, 76, 77, 86, 87
David Goldman: pages 14, 15 (below), 78, 79 (below)
Patrick Gosling: pages 52, 53
Harley-Davidson: pages 35 (below), 36
Honda UK: pages 46, 47
Mac McDiarmid: pages 7, 22, 25 (right), 26, 27, 32, 33, 42, 43, 44, 45, 51, 58, 79 (top), 88 (top), 89, 92, 93, 94, 95
Phil Masters: pages 12, 13, 17, 28, 29, 40, 41, 62, 63, 82, 83
Mitsui Yamaha: pages 84, 88 (below)
Kenny P: pages 8, 9, 66, 67, 85
Kevin Raymond: page 50
Dale Stenten: pages 20, 21
Suzuki GB: pages 68, 69, 71 (below right)
Oli Tennant: pages 5, 6, 13, 23, 24, 25, 30, 31, 37, 49, 55, 58, 59, 60, 61, 64, 65, 70, 71 (top), 80, 81, 91 (below)
to all of whom, many thanks.

Contents

Introduction 6

Nico Bakker:
QCS1000 8

Bimota:
YB11 Superleggera 10
SB6R 12
Tesi 1D 14

BMW:
K1200RS 16
R1100RS 18

Buell:
S1 Lightning 20

Cagiva:
900 Elefant 22

Ducati:
900 Monster 24
916 26
900 Superlight 32

Egli:
Egli Harley-Davidson 30

Harley-Davidson:
Dyna Glide 32
Electra Glide 34
Heritage Softail 36
XL1200S Sportster Sport 38

Honda:
F6C Valkyrie 40
CBR900RR Fireblade 42
GL1500 Gold Wing 44
VTR1000F Fire Storm 46
CBR1100XX Super Blackbird 48
RC45 50

Kawasaki:
1100 Zephyr 52
ZX-9R 54
ZX-7R 56
ZZ-R1100 58

Magni:
Australia 60

Moto Guzzi:
Centauro 62
1100 Sport Injection 64

Suzuki:
GSX-R750 66
GSF1200 Bandit 68
RF900 70
TL1000S 72

Triumph:
T595 Daytona 74
T509 Speed Triple 76
Sprint 900 78
Thunderbird 80
Trophy 1200 82

Yamaha:
FJ1200 84
YZF1000R Thunderace 86
GTS1000 88
V-Max 1200 90
XJR1200 92
YZF750 94

Index 96

Harley-Davidson Heritage Softail — proving there's sometimes more to superbikes than super performance.

Introduction

....

'A Superbike, then, is something which stands out from the common herd of two-wheelers.'

Although the word 'Superbike' didn't exist before 1969, the concept certainly did. Coined to express the sense of wonder at Honda's then new CB750-four, it might equally have been used in an earlier age to describe a Brough Superior, a Vincent Black Shadow, or even the Triumph and BSA triples which preceded the Honda by a mere year.

In some ways it is a trite expression, no more worthy of our esteem than various 'superstars' or 'supermodels'. And there is, after all, nothing very exhilarating about a 'super' market. Yet 'superbike' is also shorthand for the bewildering technical advances of motorcycling over the past 30 years. In previous times, truly outstanding machines might appear perhaps once per decade; by the early 'seventies perhaps once per year; now they're coming at us thick and fast.

So exactly what does put the 'super' into 'Superbike'? Literally, the prefix means 'above'. It can mean, and it certainly does here, 'superior in quality . . . a degree beyond the ordinary meaning'. A Superbike, then, is something set apart from the common herd of two-wheelers. It is so special that the mere words 'bike', or 'motorcycle' cannot fully fully describe it. A Superbike stands out.

It does not simply mean 'faster'. Nor does it refer to price. The very fastest and most expensive motorcycles, certainly, are Superbikes. But so are some of the slowest – at least if you allow Harley-Davidson into the equation. In their case, the 'degree extra' is some indefinable quality. It isn't simply style and it certainly isn't performance, but most motorcyclists recognise it when they see it.

That, perhaps, is the essence of the true

Honda's CBR900RR Fireblade redefined the superbike concept when launched in 1992, and still reigns supreme amongst Japanese supersport fours.

Superbike. Whatever physical properties they may have, they also possess something extra, some indefinable quality which sets them apart. Inevitably, it is subjective and open to argument. And it is by no means always the same. Whatever it is about a Harley that turns people on, Bimotas have something very different but equally desirable.

Whatever that quality might be, all the motorcycles on the following pages have it – from the sensuous good looks of Ducati's 916 to the brutal elegance of Yamaha's XJR1200. From the over-the-top specification of Honda's GL1500 Gold Wing to the sheer bruising speed of Kawasaki's ZZ-

R1100. From the stylised Retro-tech of Harley-Davidson's Heritage Softail, to the brave novelty of Bimota's Tesi 1D. From the breathtaking power-to-weight of the Honda CBR900RR Fireblade, to the understated efficiency of the BMW K1200RS.

Ironically, a common complaint about modern motorcycles is that they are 'all becoming the same'. Yet even a cursory inspection of these Superbikes reveals a mouth-watering diversity of form and function. Turn the pages, relish them, and dream. For these are not merely motorcycles, they are fantasies given physical form. 'Superbike' is really too humble a word to describe them.

Not quite the fastest, but perhaps the sexiest superbike ever built, Ducati's 916 is also almost unbeatable on the track.

Nico Bakker QCS1000

'The svelte bodywork and 'unusual' suspension systems give the QCS a look all its own.'

Only a handful of exotic bikes have single-sided suspension at even one end. Only Nico Bakker's creation boasts such technology at both.

Yamaha were the first company to put an alternative front end into mass production on a motorcycle, but they were by no means the first to experiment with replacing the front forks in favour of a better design.

One of the pioneers of alternative front ends is Dutch 'specials' builder Nico Bakker, a man with several decades of chassis and suspension building to his credit and an impressive consultancy list that includes BMW and Laverda. And his QCS1000 (QCS stands for Quick Change System – both wheels can be changed in a very short space of time) is the latest incarnation of his own very effective design.

Traditional front forks are inherently flexible and can affect a motorcycle's steering geometry as they compress in corners. A method of separating the steering from the front suspension is generally considered to be the way forward for motorcycle design, and as yet only Yamaha and BMW have put alternative front suspension systems into production. But Nico Bakker has a system which he has been using since 1988 which is both clever and effective.

The QCS is a hand-built 'special' that uses a Yamaha FZR1000 engine for its motive power, around which is wrapped an aluminium-alloy square-section chassis onto which are bolted single-sided swingarms front and back. The front suspension system works in a very similar way to that of the Yamaha GTS1000 – the steering is handled via a spar running from the hub of the front wheel to the steering crown, while the suspension is actuated by the single-sided swingarm that bolts onto the front of the chassis. The benefits of this system can best be realised by a high-performance

sportsbike, which makes Yamaha's decision to fit it to a modest-performance sports-tourer surprising.

But the performance of the QCS is anything but modest. The derestricted FZR1000 engine oozes power and torque. The five-valves-per-cylinder in-line four makes 145bhp in the QCS and is capable of whisking it up to 165mph in very short order.

The rear suspension is also a single-sided swingarm affair, but without the necessity for steering the system, is used primarily for fast wheel changes (Honda developed this system for their endurance racing bikes, and it has subsequently been used on road-going machines by Honda and Aprilia).

On the road the QCS delivers exactly what it promises. There is no front end dive when hard on the brakes, and the bike is rock-steady mid-turn. It exhibits none of the drawbacks of traditional front forks and, unlike the GTS1000, the steering response is both fast and positive. A massive front

disc brake gripped by a six-piston caliper helps stop this 160mph beast, and a massive 180/55 section rear tyre helps the QCS grip tenaciously in the corners.

The svelte bodywork and 'unusual' suspension systems give the QCS a look all of its own – the swoopy styling and bright red paint tells the world that this is one serious, and very purposeful, motorcycle.

Very much more than a mere styling exercise, the QCS combines stability and agility in unprecedented proportions.

SPECIFICATION: NICO BAKKER QCS1000	
ENGINE	Water-cooled DOHC 20-valve in-line four
DISPLACEMENT	1002cc
HORSEPOWER	145bhp @ 10,000rpm
CARBURETTORS	4 x 38mm Mikuni
GEAR BOX	Six speed
FRAME	Aluminium-alloy twin beam
WHEELBASE	57ins
WEIGHT	418lbs dry
TOP SPEED	165mph

Bimota YB11 Superleggera

The format of Bimota's YB11 Superleggera is familiar: a blend of four-cylinder Yamaha engine, twin-spar aluminium frame and top-class cycle parts. For almost a decade the Italian firm has been building Yamaha-engined fours. But none of them matches the style or the sheer performance of the YB11, which is powered by the awesome 1002cc motor from the Japanese firm's YZF1000R Thunderace.

Superleggera means 'superlight' in Italian, and the name suits Bimota's exotic flagship just fine. With its lean, aggressively sculpted styling, the YB11 looks like a more muscular, slimmed-down version of the Thunderace. At 403lbs the Bimota is 30lbs lighter than the Yamaha, and matches Honda's less powerful CBR900RR Fireblade exactly.

The YB11 certainly has heaps of pedigree. It is the latest of a long line of aluminum-framed, Yamaha-powered sportsters developed from the 750cc YB4 on which Virginio Ferrari won the Formula One world championship back in 1987. The YB6 roadster of 1988 was the first to use Yamaha's FZR1000 powerplant, and since then the big-bore motor has powered a string of Bimotas with names such as Tuatara and Furano.

Those bikes all used similar versions of the familiar twin-spar alloy frame, which was advanced in the late '80s but looks unexceptional almost ten years later. Bimota's main change for the YB11 is to relocate the main cross-member closer to the steering head, adding rigidity while slightly reducing weight.

The YB11's slim, muscular styling perfectly complements the bike's blend of light weight and potent four-cylinder engine. Compared to the Yamaha Thunderace whose powerplant it shares, the Bimota is an aggressive machine that makes very few concessions to road-riding comfort.

Even crouching as far forward as possible can't prevent the aptly-named Superleggera's front wheel from coming up when the throttle is wound open to unleash the stunning midrange power of the 20-valve Yamaha engine.

The Bimota's slim, aerodynamic bodywork and compact chassis contribute to its mind-warping acceleration and 170mph top speed. The whole bike is light, firm and superbly precise — built for speed both in corners and a straight line.

Even the standard Thunderace's thick 48mm front forks are dwarfed by the Superleggera's huge 51mm diameter stanchions. The Paioli units are adjustable for compression and rebound damping; the same Italian firm also provides the YB11's multi-adjustable rear shock.

There are no internal changes to the 20-valve, liquid-cooled Thunderace engine, which in standard form produces a claimed 145bhp at 10,000rpm. But the airbox is new and larger, fed via ducts running back from the nose of the Superleggera's sleek glass-fibre fairing. Bimota claim the airbox adds two or three horsepower in conjunction with a new four-into-one pipe and rejetting of the Yamaha's 38mm Mikuni carbs.

Although the YB11 shares its engine, chassis type and even its wheelbase with the YZF1000R, the two bikes feel distinctly different. The Bimota's suspension is firmer, its seat thinner and its riding position more racy, with hands forward, head down and feet high. By comparison Yamaha's YZF is roomy and softly sprung.

The Superleggera's reduced weight gives a slight edge to straight-line performance. A crack of the throttle sends the Bimota hammering off into the distance with its front wheel reaching for the sky. Given enough room it's good for 170mph. There's usable torque from as low as 2000rpm, and the fearsome acceleration from 5000rpm makes the YB11 an easy bike to ride very, very fast.

Although the Superleggera's race-ready suspension feels harsh on bumpy roads, on smoother surfaces the bike handles superbly, combining light steering with impeccable stability. Brembo's blend of big front brake discs and four-piston calipers gives heaps of stopping power, and Michelin's fat, grippy Hi-Sport tyres allow maximum use to be made of the YB11's almost limitless cornering clearance.

Inevitably this Bimota can't match the performance advantage that its YB6 predecessor once held over the opposition, and equally inevitably the hand-built Superleggera is horribly expensive. But with its looks, handling and outrageous performance, the YB11 is a fitting addition to Bimota's dynasty of mighty Yamaha-powered roadburners.

SPECIFICATION: BIMOTA YB11 SUPERLEGGERA	
ENGINE	Water-cooled DOHC 20-valve in-line four
DISPLACEMENT	1002cc
HORSEPOWER	148bhp @ 10,000rpm
CARBURETTORS	4 x 38mm Mikuni
GEAR BOX	Five speed
FRAME	Aluminium alloy twin beam
WHEELBASE	55.9ins
WEIGHT	403lbs dry
TOP SPEED	170mph

'The bike handles superbly, combining light steering with impeccable stability.'

Bimota SB6R

....

The SB6R's styling is subtly different to that of its SB6 predecessor. But the two bikes share a basic format of Suzuki GSX-R1100 motor in a 'Straight Connection Technology' frame, whose aluminium spars run all the way from steering head to swing-arm pivot.

Bimota's SB6R had a hard act to follow. This bike's predecessor, the SB6, was a huge success for the tiny Rimini company, selling over 1200 units in the three years following its release in 1994. Such a total is insignificant by the standards of most manufacturers – but it's enough to make the SB6 Bimota's all-time best-selling bike, so its replacement had to be good.

The SB6R is more than good, it's one of the world's great sports bikes. Rather than make dramatic changes to the SB6's format, Bimota produced the SB6R by tuning, tweaking and restyling the existing model. The extra digit supposedly stands for 'Racing', although the list of modifications adds up to a bike that is fractionally faster but, more importantly, has a slight edge over its predecessor in looks, sophistication and handling.

The basic SB6 format remains, which means that the SB6R combines the watercooled, 16-valve four-cylinder engine from Suzuki's GSX-R1100 with a short, immensely strong aluminium frame of Bimota's own design. The main frame spars run all the way from the steering head past the swing-arm pivot – hence the 'Straight Connection Technology' logo on the 6R's streamlined fibreglass fairing.

Styling is subtly different to the SB6's, from the fairing's sharper nose all the way to the carbon-fibre tailpiece, which in grand prix style is self-supporting so requires no subframe. As before, the rear shock, a multi-adjustable unit from Swedish specialist Öhlins, sits horizontally on the right of the bike. Its spring is softer than the SB6's, and has a revised rising-rate linkage.

In Bimota tradition the GSX-R engine remains internally standard, and its output is modified by

With a claimed 156bhp on tap the SB6R is awesomely fast in a straight line. It's also impressive for the way that Bimota's system of rubber-mounting the cylinder head tames the big four-cylinder Suzuki motor's vibration.

induction and exhaust modifications. New, shorter exhaust downpipes are claimed to increase power at high revs. The airbox is bigger and the 40mm Mikunis carburettors are fed by a ram-air system. Bimota chief engineer Pierluigi Marconi says the ram-air helps add a total of 10bhp, although the gain shows up only at high speed and the official maximum remains 156bhp at 10,000rpm.

Whatever the increase, the Bimota's straight-line performance is utterly fearsome. When you crack open the smooth-action throttle the SB6R flies, its torquey GSX-R motor providing shoulder-splitting midrange acceleration and a thrilling charge towards the redline. Top speed is somewhere around 170mph, and the lightweight Bimota gets there phenomenally quickly.

The SB6's rather buzzy feel at some engine speeds is notably reduced by the 6R's system of

rubber mounts where the cylinder head bolts to the frame. Other changes from the SB6 include a new vacuum fuel pump, designed to prevent the SB6's occasional starvation problems, a larger, 22-litre fuel tank, and a single battery above the airbox, instead of two hidden in the fairing nose.

Handling is subtly different to the SB6's, because the 6R's suspension has been tuned to give a slightly more compliant ride. Compression damping both in the 46mm Paioli forks and the Öhlins shock is reduced which, along with the rear unit's other changes, gives a smoother feel on bumpy roads. And although steering is quick and the 6R is short and light, its stability remains excellent.

All this, allied to racy steering geometry, the grip of fat Michelin Hi-Sport rubber and the predictably powerful bite of twin Brembo front discs with four-piston calipers, makes for a stunningly quick and deliciously agile bike. The hand-assembled Bimota's price is inevitably high, but the SB6R looks set to continue its predecessor's sales success for several years to come.

Simply sitting astride the super-light SB6R is enough to make the adrenalin start flowing — and this is no ordinary motorbike saddle. The Bimota's beautifully shaped seat unit is cut away to reveal the exhaust's twin tailpipes. In grand prix racebike fashion, the unit is a self-supporting structure made from carbon-fibre.

SPECIFICATION: BIMOTA SB6R	
ENGINE	Water-cooled DOHC 16-valve in-line four
DISPLACEMENT	1074cc
HORSEPOWER	156bhp @ 10,000rpm
CARBURETTORS	4 x 40mm Mikuni
GEAR BOX	Five speed
FRAME	Aluminium alloy twin beam
WHEELBASE	55.1ins
WEIGHT	418lbs dry
TOP SPEED	175mph

Bimota Tesi 1D

....

The Bimota Tesi is one of the most radical, extraordinary and most interesting superbikes ever built. With the Tesi, the small Italian factory took a giant leap forward in motorcycle design, one that only Yamaha (and to a lesser extent BMW) have dared to follow, although 'specials' builders such as Nico Bakker have produced similar machines in very small numbers. What Bimota did was put into production a superbike that featured hub-centre steering rather than traditional telescopic front forks.

The problem with conventional telescopic forks is that they flex under braking and cornering, and because they compress under braking, the steering geometry of the bike is altered. In an ideal world the suspension and steering of a motorcycle should be separate and independent to each other. With telescopic forks this isn't possible, no matter how good the forks are, but with hub-centre steering the suspension can be separated from the steering.

So instead of wrapping the motorcycle's engine in a conventional frame and then bolting a pair of forks to the headstock and a rear swingarm to the back, Bimota have wrapped their chassis around the sides of the engine and then bolted a swingarm on at the front and at the back. The rear swingarm pivots in the traditional way and actuates the rear shock, while the front shock is bolted to the left-hand spar of the front swingarm and to the chassis. A complicated system of linkages joins the steering column to the front wheel to allow almost 30 degrees of steering movement.

One of the advantages of using a twin-sided front swingarm (as opposed to a single-sided one like the Yamaha GTS1000) is that it allows two brake discs to be used. And with twin 320mm front discs gripped by four-piston Brembo calipers, the Tesi has one of the best brake set-ups of any superbike.

All Bimotas are beautiful. The Tesi adds technical novelty to the usual aesthetic flair of Rimini products.

'Tesi' is Italian for degree thesis — of Bimota designer Pierluigi Marconi. If only all university courses looked like this.

The engine itself is a modified version of the Ducati 904cc water-cooled eight-valve desmodromic V-twin engine which uses a development of the Weber-Marelli fuel-injection system to produce a hefty 117bhp.

If all this doesn't sound exotic enough, the whole bike is clad in carbon-fibre bodywork and equipped with a pair of Kevlar silencers. The finished result is a bike that scales a featherweight 407lbs dry and which has a wheelbase more akin to a 400cc machine than a litre bike.

On the road the Tesi is quite unlike anything else. The lack of dive when slowing, and the fact that the suspension continues to work during hard braking, means that the Tesi can be braked later and cornered harder than anything else on the road. The fire-breathing Ducati engine means that top speeds of 160mph are a breeze and that in terms of performance the Tesi will stay with the very best that Japan has to offer.

The down side is that the Tesi is a solo machine, with no accommodation for pillion passengers, and it costs twice as much as a Yamaha GTS1000. In fact, except for the Honda NR750, the Tesi is the most expensive production bike in the world. But then it is also arguably the best production bike in the world.

Unique Tesi front suspension comes into its own, howling into bumpy corners hard on the brakes.

SPECIFICATION: BIMOTA TESI 1D	
ENGINE	Water-cooled SOHC 8-valve Desmo V-twin
DISPLACEMENT	904cc
HORSEPOWER	117bhp
CARBURETTORS	Electronic fuel injection
GEAR BOX	6 speed
FRAME	Twin aluminium-alloy plates
WHEELBASE	55.5ins
WEIGHT	407lbs dry
TOP SPEED	160mph

BMW K1200RS

······························

The K1200RS is a radical bike by BMW standards, combining its 130bhp four-cylinder engine with eye-catching styling and an aluminium frame. The RS is fast, and it's also built for long-distance comfort — a sports-tourer that fully lives up to the description.

With its striking styling, aluminium frame, innovative front suspension system and powerful four-cylinder engine, BMW's K1200RS is every millimetre a modern superbike. It's also a very long way indeed from being a traditional BMW – mainly because its engine's 130bhp output blasts a huge hole in the German firm's long-held limit of 100bhp.

Even BMW's sportier models have been restrained in the past, but there is nothing dull about the K1200RS's stylishly streamlined bodywork. And nor is there anything remotely boring about the way the 16-valve RS rockets smoothly to a top speed of over 150mph.

The K1200RS is still very much a BMW, for all that. When its makers describe the RS as a sports-tourer, unlike most manufacturers they place as much emphasis on the touring side of the equation as the sports. This BMW might have plenty of speed, but it also has adjustable ergonomics, anti-lock brakes and shaft final drive.

Its engine is a revamped version of the German firm's familiar longitudinally mounted inline four, its capacity increased to 1171cc by use of a longer-stroke crankshaft. More performance is added by use of lightweight pistons and valvegear, and a higher compression ratio – all of which contribute to its peak output of 130bhp at 8750rpm.

The RS's chassis is completely new and very different to that of its K1100RS predecessor, not just because its frame is made from aluminium instead of steel, but because the engine is rubber-mounted to reduce vibration. Front suspension is by a revised version of BMW's Telelever system, which links hollow fork legs via rods to a vertically mounted shock absorber. The single-sided rear swing-arm also works a single shock, placed diagonally on the right of the bike.

Being a BMW, the RS is naturally available with numerous rider-friendly accessories including a tank-bag and panniers. The big difference between this bike and its predecessors is that even when loaded with luggage, the K1200RS is capable of cruising smoothly at 140mph.

'This is not a bike for knee-scraping cornering antics.'

What sets the RS apart from its predecessors is the exhilarating performance from its fuel-injected engine, which manages to combine its new-found high-rev power with the K-series motors' traditionally generous midrange torque. Twisting the throttle sends the big BMW storming forward almost regardless of where its tachometer needle is pointed, which makes for effortless overtaking.

Not that changing gear is a problem on the K1200RS, whose new six-speed gearbox is not just the best ever fitted to a BMW, but the first to meet Japanese standards. A slight buzz intrudes at about 4500rpm, ironically the useful 85mph-in-top-gear cruising zone. But at all other speeds the BMW feels supremely smooth and refined.

Handling is very good, too. Although, at 260kg dry, the RS is no heavier than several rival sports-tourers, it is a big machine that can be intimidating. This is not a bike for knee-scraping cornering antics; as well as the weight, it's too long, its steering geometry is too conservative and its suspension too soft.

But the RS has a pleasantly neutral and stable steering feel, excellent grip from broad radial tyres, and enough ground clearance to allow plenty of fun on a twisty road. Its Telelever front suspension eradicates fork dive under braking almost completely, soaking up bumps even when the powerful brakes – fitted with an uprated and very impressive ABS anti-lock system – are used hard.

One surprising limitation is lack of fuel capacity. The engine's thirst when used hard means that the 21-litre fuel tank gives a range of under 150 miles. But that's only a problem because the BMW is so comfortable that it allows all-day riding with no aches. If long-distance speed, comfort and style are what you require, very few bikes even come close to matching the K1200RS.

Features such as the adjustable windscreen and Telelever front suspension system are typical of BMW's innovative approach to bike design. Both work well, contributing to the way the RS swallows long distances at speed and in comfort.

SPECIFICATION: BMW K1200RS	
ENGINE	Water-cooled DOHC 16-valve longitudinal four
DISPLACEMENT	1171cc
HORSEPOWER	130bhp
CARBURETTORS	Motronic fuel-injection
GEAR BOX	Six speed
FRAME	Aluminium alloy spine
WHEELBASE	61.2ins
WEIGHT	572lbs dry
TOP SPEED	152mph

BMW R1100RS

······························

'BMW designed this bike to be a superlative sport-tourer.'

BMW have a reputation for building top-quality touring motorcycles rather than high-performance superbikes, but in recent years they have managed to bridge the gap between the two concepts. Arguably the most eye-catching of this new breed is the R1100RS.

The R1100RS is a unique departure for BMW. Since the 1930s they have been building horizontally-opposed twin-cylinder machines with two valves per cylinder actuated by push-rods. But with the R1100RS the 'Boxer' engine (as it is commonly known) has joined the latter half of the 20th Century. It is still air cooled, but the number of valves per cylinder has been doubled to four, and their camshafts are now actuated by a series of belts driven from the crankshaft.

The old Bing carburettors, always a distinctive feature of the two-valve Boxer, have also been replaced – the R1100RS is the first Boxer to feature electronic fuel-injection.

But if all that is a major departure, the innovative 'Telelever' front suspension system of the R1100RS is a quantum leap into the next century for the German marque. Just as Yamaha has looked at alternative front suspension and steering systems for motorcycles, BMW has also taken the brave step of introducing their own solution to the problem. And that problem is that ideally the steering and suspension systems for a

motorcycle's front end should be separate and independent from each other. Traditional telescopic forks flex, the steering geometry of the machine is altered when the front brake is being used, and often much of the fork's movement is taken up with braking, leaving little to deal with bumps in the road.

Yamaha's solution to the problem is the hub-centre-steered GTS1000, but BMW have taken a lower-key approach. They still use a pair of telescopic forks on the R1100RS, but they deal with the steering only. The suspension is handled by a single shock absorber bolted to the headstock and actuated by a wishbone-shaped bracket that joins the forks to the chassis. In effect the forks are merely sliders that join the front wheel to the headstock, while the wishbone actuates the shock absorber. Thus the suspension and steering are separated, creating an anti-dive effect when the front brake is applied.

This system is much simpler than that used by the Yamaha GTS1000, but is no less effective. Indeed the consensus of opinion is that the BMW

This odd-looking thing is Bavaria's answer to riders who want '90s technology in a bike they can understand.

As well as scratching well (above), the *Bee-eM* offers more user-friendly 'goodies' than practically any other motorcycle.

Boxer engine is inevitably wide (left) but the RS still has plenty of ground clearance to exploit.

Telelever system is actually more effective than that of the Yamaha. Certainly the R1100RS gives more feedback to the rider, and retains the traditional look of telescopic forks – an important consideration for the normally conservative BMW buyer.

But there's more to the R1100RS than an all-new Boxer engine and a 'funny' front end. BMW designed this bike to be a superlative sport-tourer, so comfort and the ability to cover ground effortlessly are also essential. To this end BMW have equipped the R1100RS with a host of user-friendly features that include adjustable seat height, handlebars and windscreen to enable the owner to tailor the bike to his own requirements. Hard luggage as an optional extra which, allied to a five-gallon fuel tank and a frugal 45mpg fuel consumption, means the R1100RS can cover well over 200 miles to a tankful of fuel and pack a decent amount of luggage for the two-wheeled tourist.

Weighing in at 526lb, the BMW needs good brakes, so the R1100RS has a pair of 305mm discs at the front gripped by four-piston calipers. BMW's excellent anti-lock braking system is also fitted, making this a very safe and well-braked machine. With the engine putting out 95bhp the R1100RS is capable of topping 135mph, but it is its ability to cruise all day at three-figure speeds that is its forte.

What BMW have done is build a thoroughly modern motorcycle that should appeal to the traditionalist buyer in search of something a little different. It's not the fastest machine on the roads, but it is supremely capable, and – the Bavarian hallmark – resolutely unorthodox.

SPECIFICATION: BMW R1100RS SE	
ENGINE	Air-cooled horizontally-opposed eight-valve flat twin.
DISPLACEMENT	1185cc
HORSEPOWER	95bhp @ 7250rpm
CARBURETTORS	Electronic fuel injection
GEAR BOX	Five speed
FRAME	Tubular steel
WHEELBASE	58ins
WEIGHT	526lbs wet
TOP SPEED	135mph

Buell S1 Lightning

Nothing on two wheels packs the visual punch of the Buell S1 Lightning. The barrel-chested Buell combines its big Harley-Davidson V-twin engine with a tiny seat and tail section. The result is uniquely aggressive – motorcycling's answer to the American Pit Bull terrier.

The Lightning's launch capped an exciting few years for Buell, the firm founded by Erik Buell, a former road-racer and Harley engineer. Buell made his name with a series of quick and fine-handling Harley-engined bikes such as the RR1000 and RS1200. But he was limited by lack of capital, which kept output low and prices high.

Then, in 1993, Harley-Davidson took a 49-percent stake in the renamed Buell Motorcycle Company, adding finance plus development and marketing expertise. The firm moved to a new and larger factory near Harley's base at Milwaukee, increased production to ten bikes a day, and developed several new models – the most striking of which is the Lightning.

Like previous models its engine is Harley's 1203cc Sportster unit, for the first time tuned for extra horsepower. Compression ratio is increased from 9:1 to 10:1, and breathing is improved by combining the 1200 motor's big valves with the 883cc Sportster's cylinder heads. Other changes include Screamin' Eagle camshafts, lighter flywheels and a new ignition system.

Harley's engineers were commissioned to produce a super-efficient airbox and silencer. The results, a massive black plastic airbox on the right of the bike, and an even bigger silencer running beneath the motor, are ugly but effective. Peak

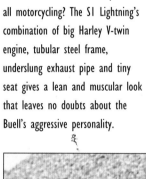

Is this the most distinctive profile in all motorcycling? The S1 Lightning's combination of big Harley V-twin engine, tubular steel frame, underslung exhaust pipe and tiny seat gives a lean and muscular look that leaves no doubts about the Buell's aggressive personality.

Erik Buell and his engineers work magic on Harley-Davidson's 1203cc V-twin engine. The Lightning produces a peak of 91bhp and delivers arm-wrenching acceleration to a top speed of 130mph. Buell's clever Uniplanar mounting system means the ride is smooth, too.

'The result is uniquely aggressive – motorcycling's answer to the American Pit Bull terrier.'

power output is 91bhp at 5800rpm, a massive 50 per cent more than a stock Sportster's figure.

The tubular steel frame is based on Buell's traditional design, with its 'Uniplanar' system of rubber mounts and rods that restrict vibration to the vertical plane. As before, suspension is by Dutch specialist WP, with 40mm upside-down forks and a single shock, situated horizontally beneath the engine and operated in tension rather than the conventional compression.

The S1 exhaust's soft, tractor-like chugging sound is disappointing, but the tacho needle races round the dial with unfamiliar enthusiasm at the blip of the throttle. At very low revs the S1 vibrates noticeably, but by 4000rpm it has cleared to give a ride as smooth as a magic carpet.

And the way the Lightning makes power is little short of amazing. The V-twin motor pulls strongly from as low as 50mph in top gear, giving a pleasantly relaxed ride. And by the short time that it takes to reach 80mph the S1 is really into its stride, living up to Buell's slogan – 'America's Faaast Motorcycle' – as it accelerates smoothly towards its 130mph top speed.

Suspension at both ends is sports-bike firm, with the 40mm WP forks doing a good job of soaking up bumps while giving a taut, racer-like feel. The rear

SPECIFICATION: BUELL S1 LIGHTNING	
ENGINE	Air-cooled pushrod OHV 4-valve 45-degree V-twin
DISPLACEMENT	1203cc
HORSEPOWER	91bhp @ 5800rpm
CARBURETTORS	40mm Keihin
GEAR BOX	Five speed
FRAME	Tubular steel ladder
WHEELBASE	55ins
WEIGHT	425lbs dry
TOP SPEED	130mph

shock is well-controlled, but harsh on rough tarmac. In combination with the tiny seat and upright riding position, that makes for an uncomfortable ride.

Other chassis parts work well. The bike can be slowed abruptly with its huge, 340mm single front disc and six-piston Performance Machine caliper, then flicked into turns quickly and fired out hard using the torque of the V-twin motor. Its Dunlop radial tyres are very grippy, and there's plenty of ground clearance.

The S1 quickly became a big hit in America, and spearheaded Buell's expansion into export markets including Japan and Europe. With its unique style, smooth performance, sharp handling and V-twin charm, the Lightning is proof that America has a serious high-performance motorcycle manufacturer at last.

Such is the Lightning's blend of acceleration and cornering power that many riders of other bikes have seen the Buell's diminutive seat and fat back tyre disappearing into the distance.

Cagiva 900 Elefant

·······················

*'As a road
bike the
Elefant is
surprisingly
capable.'*

Although based on Cagiva's successful
desert racers, the Elefant is
surprisingly adept at back-road
scratching.

The popularity of the Paris-Dakar Rally in Europe has spawned a whole generation of enormous on/off-road superbikes, and none of them is more impressive than the Cagiva 900 Elefant.

The Paris-Dakar covered thousands of miles of desert in northern Africa, and the major motorcycle manufacturers spent many years, and enormous quantities of money, building bikes that would win it. Success in the Paris-Dakar translated directly to sales in Europe.

But the demands of the Saharan marathon meant that these trailbikes had to be very big and very fast, not something normally associated with off-road bikes. They also had to be immensely rugged and capable of carrying a lot of fuel and water with them – the two-wheeled equivalent of a Landcruiser.

The Cagiva 900 Elefant is a production version of the bike which triumphed in the Paris-Dakar a few years back, and is one of the biggest and best

Paris-Dakar replicas available. It's also one of the most interesting in that it uses a 900cc air and oil-cooled overhead cam 90-degree V-twin motor with desmodromic valve gear (as used on countless Ducati road and race bikes). Electronic fuel-injection helps the Elefant to produce a healthy 70bhp at 8500rpm, although brute power is less important with this kind of off-road machine than a usable spread of torque.

A high level of suspension equipment is *de rigeur* for desert-racers, and here the Cagiva gets full marks for Marzocchi forks at the front and an Öhlins multi-adjustable monoshock at the back. Rugged long-travel suspension is a must for this type of machine, and the Elefant has it in abundance.

Hefty twin front disc brakes give the Elefant plenty of stopping power, with twin-pot Nissin calipers providing bite. A large-capacity fuel tank (although not as large as the pukka desert race

bike's) and twin-headlamp fairing are also part of the essential P-D package, as is a vertiginous seat height of over 35ins.

As a road bike the Elefant is surprisingly capable. Although lacking the kind of power to compete directly with road-going sports 900s, the Elefant has a wide spread of power and torque which makes it very usable on twisting back roads. And with a top speed of 120mph the Elefant offers plenty of thrills along the way.

But it is off-road where the Cagiva really excels. That lazy, low-revving motor and low gearing make the Elefant a superb dirt bike that is equally at home idling along narrow gravel tracks or blasting at speed across open desert. The flexibility of the V-twin engine means that gear-changes are kept to a minimum, allowing the rider to concentrate on picking the right line across whatever terrain he happens to be traversing.

The long-travel suspension soaks up all but the biggest bumps, giving a soft manageable ride under almost all road and off-road conditions. That suspension travel also makes the Elefant a comfortable long-distance road mount, too.

Although bikes like the Elefant can't offer the kind of searing performance a high-performance road-bike can, their go-anywhere, do-anything capabilities give them an appeal all their own. The Cagiva 900 is undoubtedly the pinnacle of on/off-road engineering.

Gutsy V-twin power makes stunts such as this almost second nature. But if you want wild revs, look elsewhere.

Despite bash-plate and off-road styling, 900 Elefant is more a go-anywhere tourer than a true dirt machine.

SPECIFICATION: CAGIVA 900 ELEFANT	
ENGINE	Air/oil-cooled SOHC 90-degree Desmo V-twin
DISPLACEMENT	904cc
HORSEPOWER	70bhp @ 8500rpm
CARBURETTORS	Electronic fuel-injection
GEAR BOX	Five speed
FRAME	Aluminium-alloy cradle frame
WHEELBASE	61.8ins
WEIGHT	414lbs dry
TOP SPEED	120mph

Ducati 900 Monster

'All the elements come together to make a bike that is a real pleasure to ride, and even more of a pleasure to look at.'

Ducati made their reputation by building uncompromising sports bikes for those with the discernment and money to appreciate them, but in recent years they have branched out in another direction. In late '92 Ducati unveiled the M900 Monster to a stunned public, proving that they could build exciting bikes for all tastes, not just for the race replica sports rider.

The M900 was the first Ducati for many years to appeal to a wide range of riders, from the traditional Ducati fan to the rider in search of something 'a little different'. And the Monster is certainly different. Although it uses the same engine as the Ducati 900SS, the Monster is designed to be a muscle-bike. A bike that accelerates with startling rapidity, and which is more at home cruising the urban jungle looking for traffic-light Grands Prix to take part in than jockeying for position into turn one at Monza.

The Ducati 900SS has an engine blessed with masses of low-down power and usable torque, so to make it into a serious muscle-bike Ducati lowered the gearing and slotted the engine into the steel trellis frame that is their trademark. The engine puts out 84bhp at 7000rpm, power enough to hustle the Monster to a top speed of almost 130mph. That's not all that fast for a 900cc machine, but this is a bike built for cruising and back-road riding, so there is no fairing and the riding position is very upright. That makes it great in town or on country lanes, but painful at speed on motorways.

Where the Monster is really at home is cruising the *Promenade des Anglais* in Nice or parked outside *Tre Scalini* in the *Piazza Navonna* in Rome. This is a bike for being seen on, for posing on, for getting you around town in style and comfort, and with a large grin on your face.

And that grin is there not only because the Monster is very fast from a standing-start, not only because it is equipped with the best suspension and brakes around, but because it is a stupendous-looking machine. The feel-good factor gained from

riding *Il Mostro* is enormous. Of course it does help that the Monster will out-drag all but the most powerful sports bike or supercar, that it comes with state-of-the-art 41mm upside-down forks and a multi-adjustable rear monoshock, and that it wears a massive pair of Brembo disc brakes equipped with four-piston calipers. All the elements come together to make a bike that is a real pleasure to ride, and even more of a pleasure to look at.

For the hard-core Ducati fan (a devotee of rock-solid suspension, agonising riding position, and 'idiosyncratic' electrics) the Monster will be a disappointment. But to everyone else the combination of good looks, lightning-quick steering, excellent suspension, eyeball-popping brakes and a lusty motor will ensure a huge grin and a much-depleted bank balance.

SPECIFICATION: DUCATI M900 MONSTER	
ENGINE	Air/oil-cooled SOHC 90-degree Desmo V-twin
DISPLACEMENT	904cc
HORSEPOWER	84bhp @ 7000rpm
CARBURETTORS	2 x 38mm Mikuni
GEAR BOX	Six speed
FRAME	Steel trellis
WHEELBASE	56.3ins
WEIGHT	408lbs
TOP SPEED	130mph

A rare picture of a M900 with both wheels on the ground. 'Wheelies' and 'stoppies' are more its natural territory.

Monster frame (above) comes from the 888 superbike, air-cooled engine from the familiar 900SS.

'Il Mostro' — the Monster — someone dubbed the prototype. Not surprisingly, the name stuck.

Ducati 916

....

'The spread of power is so immense that almost any gear will do.'

To many, Ducati's 916 is not merely a superbike, but *the* Superbike. Part motorcycle, part fantasy, part erotic art, few motorcycles of the past 20 years have aroused such passion amongst the motorcycling public.

Just look at it. Is there such a thing as Repetitive Strain Injury of the desire muscles? There is now. Within nanoseconds of its UK launch in late 1993, a whole generation of bikers had instantly put the 916 top of their lust list. Practically overnight, every one of the 200 destined for Britain in 1994 were sold. And the first 100 due in '95. Even at £11,800 apiece, it seemed cheap.

Not only does the 916 have looks in abundance, it has pedigree. Essentially, it is a racer, with the almost desultory addition of lights and a number plate. It is little more than a spin-off from World Superbike regulations which insist that if you can't find the same frame, engine castings and induction system in the shops, you can't put them on the track, either. For this reason, Honda would probably never have built their RC45 were it not for their Superbike racing ambitions. Ducati, on the other hand, almost certainly would have built the 916 – because they're Italian and Italians are into that sort of thing.

The 916's predecessor, the 888, had already won the World Superbike crown in 1990, '91, '92. Hot off the drawing board, the 916 followed suit, taking Carl Fogarty to memorable victory in the 1994 title chase. By the time you read this, he'll probably have won it again. And if Fogarty doesn't, another 916 almost certainly will.

Despite the leanness of its lines, the 916 is an extraordinarily complex box of tricks. That slim

SPECIFICATION: DUCATI 916	
ENGINE	Liquid-cooled DOHC 8-valve Desmo V-twin
DISPLACEMENT	916cc
HORSEPOWER	114bhp @ 9000rpm
CARBURETTORS	Programmed fuel injection, 50mm chokes
GEAR BOX	Six speed
FRAME	Tubular steel trellis
WHEELBASE	55.5ins
WEIGHT	430lbs dry
TOP SPEED	160mph

Not surprisingly, it was lust at first sight for a generation of bikers when the 916 was first unveiled. No previous machine had embodied quite the same combination of race-bred performance and sensuous good looks as the road-going counterpart of the machine which would take Carl Fogarty to his first World Superbike title.

fairing hides an engine which may 'only' be a twin, the latest in a line of Ducati V-twins dating back to 1972. But the latest Dukes have four valves per cylinder, four camshafts, six gears, liquid-cooling, computer-controlled electronic fuel injection and desmodromic valvegear.

All this advanced technology makes the 916 quite unlike most racing engines. Instead of a diet of pure, giddy revs, the twin pours out irrepressible, visceral urge almost from tickover. Solid, hard power begins as low as 3000rpm, and from 6000-upwards the universe is thrown into reverse. Top speed is a blistering 160mph.

In 955cc Superbike racing trim, the '916' develops the thick end of 150bhp. As a roadster it claims 114bhp at 9000rpm, but feels even stronger, more usable. The spread of power is so immense that almost any gear will do. And the booming roar when downshifting into corners is one of the joys of motorcycling.

The Ducati's chassis, too, is of the highest class. Compared to the 888, the 916 is shorter, more agile, more racer-like. The Japanese Showa suspension offers a huge array of settings, but there is very little wrong with the Duke straight out of the crate. With its short wheelbase and its lively geometry, it is in its element through turns – blindingly fast sweepers and hairpins alike.

Anyone buying the 916 takes custody of a dream as much as reality. As a practical street bike it has its faults, not the least of which is comfort. In a racing crouch – what it was designed for, after all – it fits like a glove. As a tourer, it makes a good plank. This is not a practical motorcycle, and every red-blooded rider in the world should want one.

Ducati 900 Superlight

'Given a crack of the throttle the Superlight thundered off.'

Red, raw and unashamedly singleminded, Ducati's 900 Superlight proved conclusively that a sports bike could provide high performance – not with excessive horsepower but through simplicity, light weight and agile handling. By modern standards the Superlight was only moderately powerful – but it was rapid, exciting and every last millimetre a pure-bred Ducati sportster.

The Superlight was launched in 1992 as a racer, more aggressive relative of the 900SS, which had been introduced in 1989 and revamped to good effect two years later. Essentially the new model was a hard-charging, single-seat version of the SS, complete with reduced weight and numerous other changes intended to cash in on Ducati's early-'90s domination of the World Superbike race series.

Most of the Superlight's 90-degree V-twin engine was derived from the 900SS, which meant it was a 904cc, single overhead camshaft unit with two valves per cylinder and desmodromic valve operation (valves closed positively, instead of by springs). The gearbox remained a six-speed unit; the only transmission difference was a ventilated cover for the Superlight's dry clutch.

The 900SS's pair of 38mm downdraft Mikunis was retained, which helped give an identical claimed peak output of 73bhp at 7000rpm. The Superlight's lack of a pillion seat allowed the free-breathing exhaust pipes to sit higher. At the other end, the new bike gained a front mudguard of lightweight carbon-fibre, instead of the conventional plastic.

In Ducati tradition the Superlight's chassis was based around a tubular steel ladder frame, and featured low-set clip-on handlebars and rearset footrests. Most of the chassis was shared with the 900SS, including the sturdy 41mm upside-down front forks from Showa, and the same Japanese firm's multi-adjustable rear shock, working directly on a cantilever swing-arm.

To that successful format the Superlight added composite wheels with aluminium rims and lightweight magnesium spokes, wearing Michelin's Hi-Sport radial tyres in suitably broad sizes. Brakes

Essentially a lightened version of the Ducati 900SS, the Superlight is a worthy descendant of the first Ducati superbikes of the mid-'seventies — lean, light and uncompromisingly purposeful.

Gutsy V-twin powerplant allows the Superlight to power hard out of bends, almost regardless of gear and revs. Handling is similarly forgiving.

were Brembo's finest: twin 320mm discs up front, gripped by four-piston Gold Line calipers.

As much as its pure performance, it was the Superlight's purposeful attitude and uncompromisingly sporty feel that made the bike so addictive. Its racy red styling, aggressive riding position and rich exhaust note gave a sporty, unmistakably V-twin feel, and the Ducati's blend of gutsy midrange torque, light weight and crisp throttle response made for a wonderfully eager and easy-to-ride machine.

That 73bhp peak output resulted in a top speed of almost 140mph, which could be bettered by several Japanese 750s. But the Ducati's combination of superlightness and broad power delivery meant the V-twin could stay with almost any competition on all but an arrow-straight road. Given a crack of the throttle the Superlight thundered off, remaining reasonably smooth all the way to its 9000rpm redline.

Handling was excellent too, thanks to the Superlight's rigid frame and its collection of top-quality cycle parts. Steering was light and neutral, giving the 388lbs Ducati the feel of a genuine middleweight. The adjustable forks gave a ride that was firm without being harsh, and the firmly sprung rear end was superbly well-controlled, even when being worked hard by the aggressive cornering encouraged by the grip of the fat and sticky rear Hi Sport tyre.

Whether the Superlight's 15lbs weight advantage, compared to the 900SS, was strictly noticeable was debatable, and the two models were certainly very

closely related in performance, as well as specification. The new bike's price was considerably higher, too. But for riders addicted to the speed, style and simplicity of Ducati's two-valves-per-cylinder V-twins, the 900 Superlight was second to none.

SPECIFICATION: DUCATI 900 SUPERLIGHT	
ENGINE	Air/oil-cooled SOHC 4-valve Desmo V-twin
DISPLACEMENT	904cc
HORSEPOWER	73bhp @ 7000rpm
CARBURETTORS	2 x 38mm Mikuni
GEAR BOX	Six speed
FRAME	Tubular steel ladder
WHEELBASE	56ins
WEIGHT	388lbs dry
TOP SPEED	137mph

Despite the fashion for aluminium beam frames, Ducati remain devoted to a steel trellis design, for the simple reason that it works.

Egli Harley-Davidson

....

'Vibration from the solidly-mounted motor added to the sensation of speed, too.'

Former Swiss racing champion Fritz Egli has been building beautifully engineered bikes around his own chassis for over 25 years. When Egli adapted his traditional steel spine frame to hold a tuned, 1607cc Harley-Davidson V-twin engine, the result was an exciting machine that was outrageous by any standards – and especially those of environment-conscious Switzerland, notorious for its strict limits on motorcycles' power and noise.

Big, basic and muscular, the first Egli Harley, built in 1992, had an aggressive and vaguely classic look, thanks to bodywork fashioned from 1960s-style unpainted aluminium. A huge petrol tank curved over the top of the grey-finished Evolution engine. Large triangular sidepanels ran below a one-and-a-half-person seat. Front and rear mudguards were also made from bare alloy sheet.

The frame consisted of a main steel spine, which doubled as the oil reservoir, plus narrower tubes that held the motor in a conventional twin cradle. Egli himself built numerous parts, including the 38mm diameter front forks and their yokes. At the rear, the triangulated steel swing-arm worked a single, multi-adjustable White Power shock absorber.

The motor was far from standard, having been built by Egli to incorporate a long list of tuning parts including Cosworth pistons, Carrillo rods and Manley valves. Plumbed with a 36mm Mikuni carburettor and an Egli-made exhaust system, the result was an increase in the V-twin's capacity from 1340cc to a massive 1607cc, raising peak output to 120bhp at 5500rpm.

When the big Harley burst into life, it did so with enough noise to start an avalanche. The view from the pilot's seat was intimidating. There was a long stretch across the alloy tank to adjustable clip-on bars that were set low and wide. Standard Harley clocks perched above the protruding fork-tops, the tacho needle flicking across the dial with every blip of the throttle.

Riding the Egli Harley confirmed that it was no docile modern sportster but a big, old-fashioned bruiser of a bike that needed a firm hand to give of its best. Its wheelbase was compact by Harley standards, at 60ins. But conservative steering geometry, an 18-inch front wheel and a high centre of gravity meant a good deal of effort was needed to change direction.

Raucous, raw and very, very rare, Fritz Egli's radical reworking of the Harley theme has more than double the power of the original.

Suspension was firm and worked well on smooth roads, the forks feeling reassuringly rigid and the well-damped rear unit keeping the back end under control. Despite its much-increased output, the engine was as tractable as any Harley motor. Crack open the throttle, and the bike hurtled forward to the accompaniment of an increasingly frenzied barrage of sound from the exhaust.

Vibration from the solidly-mounted motor added to the sensation of speed, too. Below 3000rpm the big V-twin was smooth, giving a relaxed feel up to 60mph in top gear. But the vibes arrived at that figure and increased steadily. Although the Egli stormed past 100mph on the way to a top speed of about 130mph, fast cruising was best limited to short bursts.

Rubber-mounting the engine would have been one solution – but, as Fritz Egli pointed out, much of the bike's appeal came from its raw feel, to which the untamed V-twin lump was a major contributor. At least there was no pretence with an Egli Harley. What you saw was a big, old-fashioned V-twin brute of a machine, and that was precisely what you got. Plenty of sports bikes were faster and more agile than the Egli. Few were more thrilling to ride.

SPECIFICATION: EGLI HARLEY-DAVIDSON	
ENGINE	Air-cooled pushrod OHV 45-degree V-twin
DISPLACEMENT	1607cc
HORSEPOWER	120bhp @ 5500rpm
CARBURETTORS	36mm Mikuni
GEAR BOX	Five speed
FRAME	Steel main spine and duplex cradle
WHEELBASE	60ins
WEIGHT	520lbs dry
TOP SPEED	130mph

130mph and no fairing gives the rider two choices: tuck in, or get blown away.

Steel spine frame, bespoke forks and White Power suspension still struggle to cope with a machine weighing well over 500lbs.

Harley-Davidson Dyna Glide

'The essence of any Harley is that pounding V-twin beat.'

The Dyna Glide features Harley-Davidson's latest chassis, which Harley themselves proudly claim is the result of computer-aided design (CAD). But it's a far cry from the exotic aluminium beam frames favoured by the latest Japanese race replicas. This one's steel, good ol' US steel, a direct spiritual descendant of an earlier generation of American iron horses.

Seemingly sculpted from solid billets of Milwaukee metal, Harleys spurn 'crotch rocket' styling in favour of timeless V-twin appeal. Well-spaced fork legs mark this as the 'Wide Glide' version.

But the frame is, in its modest way, a new departure for Harley-D as they progress ever-so-cautiously into the future. First seen on the 1991 Sturgis model, it features a refinement of the system of rubber engine mounting previously fitted to Glide and Low Rider models. And for the first time, it is possible for a normal person to ride a Harley at sustained speed without going numb from the wrists down.

Purists might frown. The essence of any Harley is that pounding V-twin beat. Unlike the anodyne whirr of Japanese multis, you're *supposed* to feel it. Dyna Glide's endeavour to offer the best of both worlds: you can tell there's 80 cubic inches of Milwaukee muscle down there, all right, but it doesn't put your circulation in a sling.

To ride, these are the smoothest Hogs yet, by a margin. Even sensitive souls will use power outside the Evolution engine's hitherto rev-range without worrying that the entire bike's about to fall to bits. Now you can happily ride at low revs where other Hogs quake and shudder. Or at high revs where your fillings used to be in danger of shaking out. Without laying a hand on the engine, rubber mounting has effectively widened the big Vee's powerband.

Harley themselves bill the Dynas as 'combining '70s Low Rider looks with the handling and rubber-isolated ride of today's Low Riders'. Both standard, 'Low Rider' and 'Wide Glide' models have been produced, the latter with the fork legs widely spaced. These are lean, low machines by Harley standards, styled according to whatever passes for grace in Milwaukee.

The rest, as is Harley's way, is largely in the hands of the cosmetic engineers. Using just two engines (Sporters of 883 & 1200cc, plus the 1340cc twin), and a handful of frame designs, the Milwaukee company typically produces around 20 models per year. It follows that many of the differences are cosmetic, and there are truly only four types of Harley: Sportsters, Low Riders, Softails and Glides. Dyna Glides are essentially a variation of the Low Rider theme.

This is precisely the point. Whilst owners of European and Japanese sports machines might discuss the number of valves per cylinder, or the thousands of suspension options available, Harley owners are interested in style. If it's paint, badging, chrome or tassels, Harley can supply it from a bewildering accessory list. And if they can't, an entire industry of custom goodies manufacturers will be happy to oblige.

Equally, whilst outright performance is rarely at the top of any Harley owner's shopping list, mild performance options are popular. Again, there's a Harley catalogue of bolt-on 'Screaming Eagle' parts.

Such are the number of variables that it's impossible to describe in detail how any particular model performs: on the whim of the stylists different Dyna Glides, for instance, feature one or two front disc brakes. So some stop, and some don't. Dyna Wide Glide's have poor ground clearance, even by Harley standards. Others are adequate, just about.

Inescapably, functionality is not the point. It's how a Harley looks that makes it Super. Beauty might be in the eye of the beholder, but nothing turns heads quite like a Hog.

SPECIFICATION:	HARLEY-DAVIDSON DYNA GLIDE
ENGINE	Air-cooled OHV 45-degree V-twin
DISPLACEMENT	1340cc
HORSEPOWER	55bhp @ 5000rpm
CARBURETTORS	40mm Keihin
GEAR BOX	Five speed
FRAME	Tubular steel twin cradle
WHEELBASE	65.5in
WEIGHT	599lb
TOP SPEED	105mph

Upper digits of speedo are redundant, but on a Hog it's style, not speed, that counts.

Unmistakably 'born in the USA', but modern rubber-mounting of the engine insulates the rider from the shuddering twin's customary vibes.

Harley-Davidson Electra Glide

The Electra Glide has to be one of the most famous names in motorcycling. Ask anyone to name a make and model of motorcycle and the chances are they'll say Harley-Davidson Electra Glide. Immortalised by the film *Electra Glide in Blue*, and by the California Highway Patrol, the Electra Glide is the archetypal American superbike.

The Electra Glide has been around for 30 years, and has remained pretty much unchanged during that time. Harley-Davidsons aren't renowned for their speed or sporting prowess, and the Electra Glide is no exception. Using a large-capacity but low-revving V-twin engine, the Electra Glide is built for comfort rather than speed.

The engine is something of a curiosity in the motorcycle world these days – people just don't build 1340cc air-cooled push-rod V-twins anymore. With increasingly stringent noise and emissions regulations being put in place by governments around the world, the future of the traditional Harley engine looks rather bleak. But until the day arrives when they can't get through the homologation procedures, the big twins will continue to delight their fans.

Harley-Davidsons have been described as being as high-tech as a mangle, and although that is somewhat overstating the case, the appeal of Harleys is their simplicity. That, and their classic

'Undoubtedly gorgeous-looking machines, Harleys have become a cult icon.'

Possibly the biggest item of designer jewellery ever created, the Electra Glide legend rumbles on and on.

The wheels of choice for film stars and rock legends, but the 'Glide is also the Stateside tourer *par excellence*.

good looks. Undoubtedly gorgeous-looking machines, Harleys have become a cult icon. Not all that long ago the Harley was the mount of the outlaw biker, but these days the Harley rider is more likely to be a stockbroker, film star or rock legend. Harleys have become the chic and expensive playthings of the rich and famous.

So what is the Electra Glide like? The engine is a vast unit, heavily over-engineered and built to last a life-time. Although it displaces 1340cc it produces a meagre 55bhp, allowing the Electra Glide to rumble to a top speed of around 110mph. That's not what you'd call fast, but the engine is blessed with an abundance of torque that means you put it in top gear and allow the motor to chug away in its own leisurely way.

The thing to remember about Harleys is they were designed for use in the USA, where 65mph is as fast as you can go and where the distances are huge. For this reason the Electra Glide is designed to cover ground slowly but effortlessly. Unlike machines such as the Honda Gold Wing, which bristle with state-of-the-art electrical gizmos, the Electra Glide relies on soft suspension, a plush seat, and a low-revving engine to make it a fine long-distance tourer. And a very accomplished tourer it is – it will cover 200 miles without having to stop for fuel, and when you do stop you aren't suffering the aches and pains experienced with some other touring machines.

Harleys have never had good brakes, high-tech suspension, or any of the other things the

Japanese, British, German or Italian motorcycle manufacturers use to make their machine better than anyone else's. Instead, Harleys are built to a competent level and the Harley image and name does the rest. The fact that they look fantastic and are very desirable means that Harley-Davidson sell every one they make without any effort at all. The Electra Glide might not be fast, it might not be powerful, but it is certainly one of the most stylish and prestigious superbikes around today.

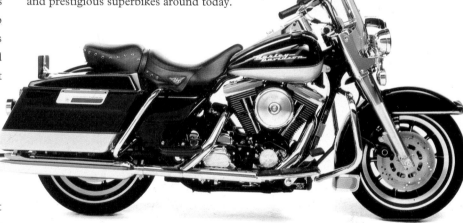

Only something this big could make 1340cc of air-cooled twin appear dainty.

SPECIFICATION: HARLEY-DAVIDSON ELECTRA GLIDE	
ENGINE	Air-cooled OHV 45-degree V-twin
DISPLACEMENT	1340cc
HORSEPOWER	55bhp @ 5000rpm
CARBURETTORS	40mm Keihin
GEAR BOX	Five speed
FRAME	Steel double-cradle
WHEELBASE	62.9ins
WEIGHT	741lbs dry
TOP SPEED	110mph

Harley-Davidson Heritage Softail

'Not for Harley the headlong race for performance.'

Despite rumours to the contrary, with the Softail, nostalgia definitely *is* what it used to be – or as near as Harley can make it. And very lucratively so.

Nostalgia, as they say, isn't what it used to be. It's better. For this, ladies and gentlemen, is Retro-tech. It is Harley-Davidson's shatteringly successful attempt to sell back to the motorcycling public those dreamy days of the 'fifties when the sun always shone and the Platters presided over a million teenage romances.

Not for Harley the headlong race for performance. Of overhead camshafts, they have none. Two valves per cylinder is all you get, and liquid-cooling is strictly for cars. What you get instead is style, American-style, in huge imposing motorcycles deliberately engineered to ape a bygone age: Retro-tech.

Although the Glide range has now evolved into something distinct (see page 36), the Heritage Softail is not unlike the original Glide, the Hydra-Glide of 1949. This was the first Milwaukee machine to feature telescopic forks, and the Softail's are shrouded to emulate the earlier design.

Glides didn't boast swing-arm rear suspension until the Duo-Glide of 1958. A cursory inspection of any Softail suggests that it, too, is a pre-'58 design. But what the designers have done is style a rear suspension which looks 'hardtail', but is in fact fully sprung. A pair of damper units reside discreetly under the gearbox as though ashamed to own up to the 1990s. This is 'Softail' and, like most things Harley, even the name is copyright.

Between '49-style forks and the *appearance* of no rear suspension is slung the classic Harley V-twin. Like the chassis, on first examination it could have been built pretty well any time between 1920 and the present. But yet again, appearances are deceptive. This is a 1340cc 'Evolution' unit, dating from 1985. Modernisation has improved reliability, without sacrificing the V-twin's classic charm.

All these things the Heritage has in common with the rest of the Softail range – the 'standard' Softail Custom and the Fat Boy. The Springer Softail goes even further down the retro route in wearing forks which mimic '30s girders. All are massive machines – the lightest is 617lbs – with distinctly modest power outputs, and the power-to-weight of a not very sporting car. Cruising, not scratching, is where Softails are at.

So riding any Harley is more a spiritual experience than an adrenaline-soaked thrill. The Heritage Softail, arguably the biggest fashion accessory in the world, takes this to extremes. It rolls around amiably on its ponderously fat tyres, vibrates like mad at any sort of revs and changes gear only in its own good time.

Since, unlike Glides, Softail engines are not rubber-mounted, vibration is acute at high revs. You're never left in any doubt that the shuddering lump under the petrol tank is a real engine producing prodigious torque at low revs, the two-wheeled equivalent of generations of Detroit V-eights. This, more than anything else, is a Harley's soul.

The rear suspension, meanwhile, is better than it looks without actually being much good. Despite the constraints inherent in the styling, Softails in fact boast more rear suspension travel – 4.06in – than any other models in the Harley range. But hit something hard, and you'd better hope your vertebrae are in good shape. Braking is similarly feeble by current standards. It is actually possible to lock a Softail

front wheel, but you need a helluva fright to work up the necessary energy. Like all Harleys, you use plenty of rear brake to slow down.

But slow and stately is the point. Legends, after all, are not to be hurried.

SPECIFICATION:	HARLEY-DAVIDSON HERITAGE SOFTAIL
ENGINE	Air-cooled OHV 45-degree V-twin
DISPLACEMENT	1340cc
HORSEPOWER	55bhp @ 5000rpm
CARBURETTORS	40mm Keihin
GEAR BOX	Five speed
FRAME	Tubular steel twin cradle
WHEELBASE	62.5in
WEIGHT	710lb
TOP SPEED	105mph

Cruisin' is what Harleys do best, whether loping across the American Prairies or ambling along English country lanes.

Lazy, low-revving 'Evolution' engine has deservedly banished the reputation Harleys once had for unreliability.

Harley-Davidson
XL1200S Sportster Sport

Harley-Davidson's Sportster is a rolling, rumbling two-wheeled legend – but it's one that hasn't lived up to its name for many years. Shortly after its launch back in 1957, the lean, tuned-up 883cc V-twin really was a sports machine, boasting 110mph top speed, fierce acceleration and respectable handling. But then the Sportster was outpaced first by British twins and then by Japanese multis, changing little in style or performance as its name became less apt with every passing year.

That hasn't prevented Harley's most basic bike from remaining hugely popular right up to the present day. Thanks largely to its good looks, character and competitive price, the Sportster has often been the best-selling motorcycle on the American market. And in 1996, Harley's

management gave the bike back a little of its ancestors' aggression by producing the XL1200S Sportster Sport – the closest thing to a truly sporty Sportster for years.

The key to the Sportster Sport is its considerably uprated chassis. Its Showa 39mm front forks and twin rear shocks are fully adjustable for preload, compression and rebound damping – a major first for Harley. The front brake features not one but two drilled 292mm floating discs, and is bolted to a cast wheel which, like its rear counterpart, wears a wide radial tyre. Compared to the cycle parts worn by previous Sportsters, this is serious stuff.

Much of the rest of the bike is familiar, including the faithful 1203cc, aircooled 45-degree motor whose only change is a revamp to the five-

The profile is classical Sportster: raised bars, peanut gas tank and V-twin motor with 'staggered shorty dual' pipes. But this is the sportiest Sportster yet – thanks to uprated, multi-adjustable suspension, twin floating front disc brakes and sticky radial tyres. Handling, roadholding and braking are still a long way from grand prix standard – but this Harley is a whole lot of fun on a twisty road.

The Sportster Sport's peak output is little more than 50bhp, but there's a fair amount of midrange torque and the Harley has more than enough power to lift its front wheel when the occasion demands.

'The Harley trundles up to about 120mph given enough time.'

speed gearbox, aimed largely at reducing noise. That means the aircooled, pushrod-operated motor's peak output remains somewhere in the modest mid-50bhp range, delivered at about 5000rpm.

Straight-line performance is unchanged from other recent 1200 Sportsters. The XL pulls cleanly at low revs and rumbles easily along with a pleasantly laid-back feel at legal speeds, accelerating crisply until it's cruising quite smoothly at 70mph with just 3000rpm showing on the tacho. At fairly slow speeds the upright riding position is comfortable, and the gearbox allows easy short-shifting to make the most of the strong low-rev performance.

Inevitably the Harley is less impressive when revved harder, beginning to vibrate noticeably by 4000rpm. By 5000rpm there's a fair amount of buzzing coming through the handlebars. The Harley trundles up to about 120mph given enough time, but it's a tough rider who can hold high cruising speeds for long.

If this Sportster's engine performance remains much the same as ever, then happily that's not true of its chassis. This is still a basic and old-fashioned motorbike, with a simple twin-cradle steel frame, a 19-inch front wheel and a substantial 497lbs of weight. But its chassis parts are an improvement on anything that Harley has previously fitted.

Most noticeable is the front brake, which despite its feeble-looking single-action calipers gives very respectable stopping power. The grippy Dunlop tyres fitted as standard are well up to coping with this, and combine with the Sport's reasonably generous ground clearance to allow lots of fun on a twisty road. Most important, though, is the Harley's uprated suspension, which is comfortable on its standard settings in town – and can be fine-tuned to give more control for hard riding.

Even these modifications and the Sportster Sport name do not make this Harley a genuine high-performance motorcycle. But the charismatic V-twin remains as stylish and as endearingly simple as ever, and the 1200S handles and stops well enough to make for an entertaining twisty-road ride. It's the best Sportster yet, and is sure to help the legendary name rumble on for many more years to come.

Harley's 1203cc, 45-degree V-twin powerplant is cooled by air and operates its valves via pushrods, just like its predecessors. This motor has a revised five-speed gearbox, but the Sportster Sport's extra performance comes from its chassis.

SPECIFICATION:	HARLEY-DAVIDSON XL1200S SPORTSTER SPORT
ENGINE	Air-cooled OHV 4-valve 45-degree V-twin
DISPLACEMENT	1203cc
HORSEPOWER	55bhp @ 5000rpm
CARBURETTORS	40mm Keihin
GEAR BOX	Five speed
FRAME	Tubular steel duplex cradle
WHEELBASE	60.2ins
WEIGHT	497lbs dry
TOP SPEED	120mph

Honda F6C Valkyrie

....

Honda's F6C is quite simply the most surprising superbike of recent years. At first sight the gigantic, chrome-covered, six-cylinder F6C looks more like a two-wheeled burger bar than a serious motorcycle. But looks can be deceiving. One ride on the improbably fast and agile Honda is guaranteed to put a helmet-splitting grin on the face of even the most sceptical rider.

The F6C is built in America (where it is known, rather more imaginatively, as the Valkyrie) and is Honda's attempt to create a new two-wheeled category: the 'performance cruiser'. That meant combining the all-American style of high handlebars, big fenders and fat tyres with the sort of performance more commonly associated with low bars and streamlined fairings.

Honda's engineers were determined that the bike should be stamped with the Japanese marque's own identity, so they utilised the 1520cc flat-six engine of the legendary Gold Wing tourer. The motor is tuned slightly with hotter camshafts, a new exhaust system and six carbs in place of the Wing's two. The result is a maximum power output of 100bhp – heady stuff by cruiser standards – and generous torque production from very low revs.

The shaft-drive motor sits in a tubular steel frame developed from that of the Wing. Suspension is seriously heavy-duty, with massive 45mm upside-down forks up front. A pair of chrome-covered rear shocks holds up the back end of a bike which, at almost 700lbs dry, is heavy even for a giant cruiser.

Happily the F6C is far more manageable than

With its outrageous combination of cruiser styling, huge flat-six engine and remarkably capable chassis, the Valkyrie is a motorcycle like nothing else on two wheels. Predictably it has been a big success in the American market, where cruisers dominate and Honda's six-cylinder Gold Wing is a legend.

'The F6C will happily cruise at over 100mph until your neck muscles have had enough.'

For such a big bike the F6C handles amazingly well. It stays stable right up to its top speed of almost 130mph. And despite its weight, it corners well thanks to fairly firm and well-damped suspension, adequate ground clearance and grippy tyres.

its size and spec sheet suggest. The bike's low centre of gravity, conservative steering geometry and long wheelbase combine to provide a solid feel. The wide bars help give reasonably light steering, allowing easy slow-speed manoeuvring.

The big bike's user-friendly feel is also due to its engine, which is just about the most flexible powerplant ever suspended between two wheels. The Valkyrie has so much low-down grunt that it barely needs a gearbox at all. On this bike you often find yourself short-shifting into top at just 2000rpm, and when requested the big six will pull from much lower than that.

Yet the Valkyrie very much lives up to its billing as a 'performance cruiser' too. Keep the tacho needle flicking towards the 6500rpm redline, and

the six is a seriously rapid motorcycle. Top speed is over 125mph, and the F6C will happily cruise at over 100mph until your neck muscles have had enough.

If the engine's performance is impressive, the fact that the chassis encourages you to use it is even more so. The Honda remains stable at speed despite all its weight, and its suspension is good enough to make quick cornering not only possible but enjoyable. The Valkyrie gives a slightly less plush ride than many cruisers but it can be banked into a bend with real confidence.

The Honda's Dunlop radials grip well and are certainly wide – the 180-section rear is as fat as most superbike tyres. Ground clearance is generous by cruiser standards, too. And the F6C has plenty of braking power, thanks to twin discs up front plus a slightly larger disc at the rear.

Of course the big, heavy six still has limitations as a performance machine, but it's impossible not to be impressed by the way it goes about its business. The F6C blends distinctive looks with a smooth, powerful, supremely flexible engine and a remarkably good chassis. Honda set out to build a giant cruiser with the performance to match its size – and they succeeded handsomely.

The Valkyrie's 1520cc flat-six powerplant produces an impressive maximum of 100bhp, but it's the Honda's low-rev torque that takes its rider's breath away. Simply winding open the throttle at almost any engine speed sends the big Six surging smoothly forward.

SPECIFICATION: HONDA F6C VALKYRIE	
ENGINE	Water-cooled SOHC 12-valve flat six
DISPLACEMENT	1520cc
HORSEPOWER	100bhp @ 6000rpm
CARBURETTORS	6 x 28mm Keihin
GEAR BOX	Five speed
FRAME	Tubular steel cradle
WHEELBASE	66.5ins
WEIGHT	682lbs dry
TOP SPEED	128mph

Honda CBR900RR
Fireblade

·····························

The Fireblade is simply the superbike by which all others are currently judged. At the cutting-edge of superbike technology, the Fireblade combines superlative performance with light weight and peerless handling to create a bike that many have tried to imitate but none has equalled.

Motorcycle manufacturers love to announce 'revolutionary new concepts' in motorcycle design, but realistically few of them ever come up with any such thing. Yet the Fireblade is one such machine. Launched in 1992, it re-wrote the rule book for performance motorcycles, combining litre bike power in a package the size and weight of a 600. Overnight, the rest of the supersport litre bike class became dinosaurs. What previously was thought to be the pinnacle of motorcycle performance was suddenly rendered obsolete.

So what makes the Fireblade so special? Very simply, it is the combination of a powerful engine in a small, lightweight machine, fitted with state-of-the-art suspension and brakes. The engine itself is nothing exceptional, being a very familiar water-cooled DOHC 16-valve in-line four putting out 125bhp – pretty much the industry standard for a 1000cc machine.

The chassis is an aluminium-alloy beam, again an industry standard in the supersports category, with a pair of hefty 45mm telescopic forks at the front and a multi-adjustable rising-rate monoshock at the back. Interestingly, Honda ignored the current trend for fitting inverted telescopic forks and a 17-inch front wheel to the Fireblade, instead opting for ordinary telescopic forks and a 16-inch wheel. Brakes are a pair of 296mm discs at the front

Britain's best-selling superbike packs a heavyweight punch into a middleweight parcel. When launched in 1992, it re-wrote the rules.

'The nature of the Fireblade means that this is not a bike for the faint-hearted or for the touring motorcyclist.'

with four-piston calipers, and a single 240mm disc at the back.

Looking at the specification sheet of the Fireblade, it's hard to work out quite why this is such an exceptional motorcycle. The sum of the parts doesn't seem to add up to anything more than what is on offer from the other manufacturers of superbikes, yet in use the Fireblade stands head and shoulders above everything except the priciest hand-built exotica from Italy.

On the road the Fireblade is so light and so nimble it feels like a race-bred middleweight, yet it packs the punch of a bike from the heavyweight division. The steering response is razor-sharp and allows the Fireblade to be flicked through corners at tremendous speed and with absolute precision. Although the Fireblade may not be the fastest bike on the roads (a top-speed of 165mph is a good 10mph down on machines like the Kawasaki ZZ-R1100), it is almost certainly the fastest bike point-to-point. The ease with which it corners, brakes and accelerates means that off the motorway there's nothing to touch it (except another Fireblade).

The nature of the Fireblade means that this is not a bike for the faint-hearted or for the touring motorcyclist. It is cramped and not at all comfortable, nor is it very practical. But for pure, hedonistic motorcycling at the very edge of the performance envelope there isn't much that comes close.

The Fireblade has raised superbike performance to a level now where the only limits are those of the rider rather than those of the machine. Motorcycle manufacturers will continue to produce better and better machines, but the Fireblade will be remembered as the bike that brought perfection to the masses, and at an affordable price.

SPECIFICATION: HONDA FIREBLADE	
ENGINE	Liquid-cooled DOHC 16-valve in-line four
DISPLACEMENT	893cc
HORSEPOWER	124bhp @ 11000rpm
CARBURETTORS	4 x 38mm Keihin CV
GEAR BOX	Six speed
FRAME	Aluminium-alloy twin beam
WHEELBASE	55.3ins
WEIGHT	407lbs dry
TOP SPEED	165mph

Searing acceleration makes keeping the front wheel down the hardest trick in the Fireblade book.

Honda GL1500 Gold Wing

'On the open road the Gold Wing performs faultlessly, as long as you never forget it weighs 800lbs and isn't designed as a sportsbike.'

When it comes to sheer size, superbikes don't come any bigger than Honda's GL1500 Gold Wing. This leviathan of the two-wheeled world is the ultimate in motorcycling comfort, designed solely to transport two people in as much style and luxury as is possible.

The Gold Wing has been around for two decades, during which time it has evolved from a fairly basic naked tourer into an everything-but-the-kitchen-sink machine for the discerning traveller. It began life as a 1000cc flat-four, grew to an 1100cc flat-four, a 1200cc flat-four, and finally into a 1500cc flat-six.

Yes, six cylinders power this mighty beast, producing 98bhp at 5200rpm and a massive 110ft/lb of torque at 4000rpm. Despite weighing in at a hefty 800lbs dry, the 'Wing is capable of a top speed of 130mph, although it takes its time getting there.

But top speed isn't what the Gold Wing is about. Smooth, effortless power delivery, luggage-carrying capacity, and supreme comfort, are what the Gold Wing is all about. And it is justly famous for achieving its purpose. The barn-door-like fairing is large enough to keep the wind and rain off the rider (although internal vents in the fairing allow you to direct cooling air at yourself when the weather gets hot). The saddle is a masterpiece of the furniture-makers art, coddling the behinds of rider and pillion, and adding to the almost total absence of vibrations from the engine to give the smoothest ride known to motorcycling.

Further to enhance the comfort and quality of ride, an on-board air-compressor allows the rider to pump up the rear suspension, and the adjustable

windscreen allows riders of any height the optimum view of the road ahead. Cruise-control is a prerequisite on this kind of bike (designed, as it is, primarily for the US market where speeds are low but sustainable for hours on end), and the Gold Wing has an effective and easy-to-use one.

But the *pièce de résistance* is the Gold Wing's sound system. The radio-cassette player is an amazing piece of technology that allows you to listen to your favourite music as you cruise the highways. Even at three-figure speeds the stereo system is clearly audible thanks to the sensor that automatically adjusts the volume to compensate for ambient wind noise.

When it comes to transporting your belongings, the Gold Wing is similarly impressive. The panniers and top-box will swallow huge amounts of luggage, and the top-box even boasts an interior light and vanity mirror!

On the open road the Gold Wing performs faultlessly, as long as you never forget it weighs 800lbs and isn't designed as a sportsbike. Fully-loaded the 'Wing will cruise all day at 90mph while you and your passenger sit comfortably behind the huge fairing listening to your favourite radio programme. With a range of over 200 miles from a tankful of fuel the 'Wing can cover 1000 miles in a day with ease, and still leave the rider fresh enough to do the same again the next day. And the day after that.

And that is the sole purpose of the Gold Wing, to make travelling by motorcycle as comfortable and pleasant as possible. It doesn't offer adrenaline-pumping speed or svelte good looks, it just makes touring a uniquely majestic experience.

SPECIFICATION: HONDA GOLD WING	
ENGINE	Water-cooled SOHC horizontally-opposed flat-six
DISPLACEMENT	1520cc
HORSEPOWER	98bhp @ 5200rpm
CARBURETTORS	2 x 33mm Keihn
GEAR BOX	Five speed
FRAME	Steel double-cradle
WHEELBASE	67ins
WEIGHT	798lbs dry
TOP SPEED	130mph

More dials and gizmos than IBM's latest, the 'Wing offers creature comforts few living rooms can equal.

The only 'six' still in production, the low-tuned Boxer engine offers effortless torque at almost any revs.

Honda VTR 1000F Fire Storm

'Its riding position is sporty without putting too much weight on the wrists.'

With its combination of torquey 996cc motor and agile yet stable handling, the FireStorm rapidly made its mark as the most practical large-capacity V-twin sportster. Some riders thought its styling bland, but the twin side-mounted radiators provided evidence of clever and original design.

Like Honda's ever-popular VFR750F, the FireStorm is designed to be sporty yet also comfortable. With an efficient half-fairing, not-too-radical riding position and compliant suspension, the VTR can cover long distances effortlessly — yet it also has the sheer performance of a much more singleminded superbike.

Honda's VTR1000F FireStorm is so rapid, so capable and above all so much fun to ride that it begs one simple question: why did the world's largest motorcycle manufacturer take such a long time to build its first big V-twin sports bike? The distinctive character and user-friendly power delivery of the VTR, coupled with its compact size and light weight, made the twin seem a natural part of Honda's range from the moment it was launched.

Unlike Suzuki's TL1000S, which appeared simultaneously, the FireStorm is not a singleminded super-sports machine built to trade blows with Ducati's 916. Instead the VTR is a sporty yet versatile superbike that is more in the style of Honda's own VFR750F. Yet it's a machine which, despite a degree of compromise in its design, is capable of running with the fast crowd too.

The VTR engine shares its watercooled, 90-degree layout and even its bore and stroke dimensions and 996cc capacity with the TL1000S, but in other respects the two motors are very different. Instead of fuel-injection the Honda uses twin 48mm Keihin carburettors. And that big eight-valve motor is tuned for midrange torque as much as for top-end power, developing a respectable peak output of 110bhp at 9000rpm, but impressing even more with its healthy output at lower engine speeds.

Its chassis is conventional, being based on an aluminium beam frame that is most notable for holding novel side-mounted radiators, which are used to free up space in front of the engine. Suspension is a typical Honda blend of 41mm conventional front forks and Prolink monoshock rear. Styling is pleasant without being particularly exciting – but any complaints about that disappear the moment you pull away.

The FireStorm's most memorable characteristic is that midrange power delivery, which makes the big Honda a hugely easy and enjoyable bike to ride very fast indeed. Winding open the throttle with the tacho needle anywhere between 2000 and 7000rpm sends the V-twin surging smoothly forward, providing relaxed yet swift top-gear travel. At higher revs the 'Storm starts to run out of breath, but it keeps pulling to the 9500rpm redline in the lower gears, and to a top speed of about 160mph.

The Honda's user-friendly power characteristics are perfectly complimented by its chassis, which gives light steering and stable handling without approaching the razor-sharp feel of an out-and-out super-sports bike. Relatively conservative chassis geometry and a fairly long wheelbase mean that the VTR isn't quite as agile as some rivals on a twisty road, but it gains by remaining stable in situations that would upset more racy machines.

Part of the reason for that is the Honda's suspension, which is slightly soft for ultra-hard riding, but has enough damping to keep control on a bumpy road. For less than flat-out riding the FireStorm gains by being quite comfortable, too. Its riding position is sporty without putting too much weight on the wrists, even when the powerful Nissin front brakes are used to the full. The half-fairing is reasonably protective, and the footpegs allow a fair amount of legroom without compromising ground clearance.

Mention of comfort should not detract from the VTR's outright performance, particularly as back-to-back tests have shown that in some situations the Honda's stability and broad power-band actually

SPECIFICATION: HONDA VTR1000F
FIRESTORM

ENGINE	Water-cooled DOHC 8-valve
	90-degree V-twin
DISPLACEMENT	996cc
HORSEPOWER	110bhp @ 9000rpm
CARBURETTORS	2 x 48mm Keihin
GEAR BOX	Six speed
FRAME	Aluminium alloy twin beam
WHEELBASE	56.3ins
WEIGHT	422lbs dry
TOP SPEED	160mph

make the bike faster than its more singleminded
rivals. The FireStorm's competitive price makes a
great bike seem even more attractive. This might be
Honda's first big V-twin sportster, but it certainly
won't be the last.

Honda CBR1100XX Super Blackbird

Honda's aim with the CBR1100XX Super Blackbird was crystal clear: to build the world's fastest production motorcycle. For five years the world's largest bike manufacturer looked on while Kawasaki's 175mph ZZ-R1100 held that unofficial title. In designing a new four-cylinder flagship, Honda's engineers were determined to capture the crown.

And with the Super Blackbird, they did just that. When the CBR1100XX was released in late 1996, it did not quite succeed in matching the pre-launch publicity that had estimated its top speed at close to 190mph. But the Blackbird – named after an ultra-rapid American spy-plane – was Super enough, flying to 180mph thanks to slippery aerodynamics and a supremely powerful engine.

Honda's mission was accomplished; Kawasaki were pushed back to second place. That fact alone was enough to ensure the Honda's impact, although in other respects the CBR1100XX – which, like the ZZ-R1100, was more of a sports-tourer than a pure-bred sports machine – is far less outrageous than its specification suggests.

That is certainly true of its styling, which was designed for aerodynamic efficiency rather than looks. The slim fairing, whose shark-like pointed nose was achieved by placing the headlight's twin lenses one above the other (rather than side-by-side as normal), helps give a remarkably low drag coefficient. But the bike's appearance is restrained, thanks partly to paint schemes of grey, black or dark red.

The Super Blackbird's straight-line performance is truly memorable, but the same can't be said of the Honda's thoroughly anonymous looks. The polite way of describing the CBR1100XX's appearance is to say that aerodynamic efficiency took precedence over eye-catching styling when the bike was being designed.

Honda's pre-launch claims that the Super Blackbird would manage 300km/h – over 185mph – proved optimistic, but the CBR is a mighty fast motorbike nevertheless. With rider's head tucked behind the screen, it's good for a genuine 180mph.

'The furnace-like power unit is the Blackbird's undoubted star attraction.'

Although the Blackbird's peak output of 162bhp at 10,000rpm is exceptional, the 1137cc motor itself is a thoroughly conventional liquid-cooled, 16-valve twin-cam four. Its most novel feature is the inclusion of not one but two balancer shafts, which make the engine so smooth that it is able to aid chassis rigidity by being solidly mounted in the aluminium twin-beam frame.

The furnace-like power unit is the Blackbird's undoubted star attraction, producing a violent surge of acceleration when the throttle is opened anywhere between 5000rpm and the 10,800rpm redline. The Honda is typically sweet and refined at low revs, too, although it has a slight flat-spot at 4000rpm that can hinder top-gear overtaking.

Handling is excellent, although this CBR is no lightweight rival for Honda's CBR900RR Fireblade. The Blackbird's longish wheelbase and 491lbs of weight mean that it's more suited to high-speed motorway travel than to scratching round a

racetrack. Straight-line stability is flawless; steering reasonably light; suspension compliant and well-damped.

The Blackbird's braking system incorporates the latest update of Honda's Dual-CBS system, as used by the CBR1000F, which applies balanced force to front and rear discs when either the hand lever or foot pedal is activated. Many riders rate the system highly, although others prefer the more direct feel of a good conventional set-up.

In contrast to the ultra-sporty Fireblade, the Blackbird incorporates a number of rider-friendly details such as a clock and fuel gauge in the dashboard, a broad dual-seat with pillion grab-rail, and clear mirrors that hold the indicators. The low screen, designed to boost top speed, is less impressive. It directs wind straight at a normally seated pilot's head, generating noise at speed.

That detracts from the Super Blackbird's efficiency as an all-round superbike, and there is no doubt that Honda were forced to make some compromises in the search for big numbers. Despite that, though, the CBR1100XX outperforms the ZZ-R1100 in most key areas. And in the one that matters most – top speed – the Super Blackbird succeeds in putting Honda on top of the world.

The Blackbird's fairing and front mudguard are shaped to keep airflow as smooth as possible. The headlight's lenses are set one above the other, instead of side-by-side as normal, to reduce width.

SPECIFICATION: HONDA CBR1100XX SUPER BLACKBIRD	
ENGINE	Water-cooled DOHC 16-valve in-line four
DISPLACEMENT	1137cc
HORSEPOWER	162bhp @ 10,000rpm
CARBURETTORS	4 x 42mm Keihin
GEAR BOX	Six speed
FRAME	Aluminium alloy beam
WHEELBASE	58.7ins
WEIGHT	491lbs dry
TOP SPEED	180mph

Honda RC45

·······················

'Racers and road riders alike queued up to place their orders for the new bike.'

This is very much more than a motorcycle. This is Honda's attempt to wrest world superbike dominance back from Ducati and Kawasaki. The result simply bristles with high technology.

Honda's RC30 was a tough act to follow. It had firmly established itself as one of the all-time great race bikes, and was also a favourite amongst discerning (and well-off) road riders. But by 1993 it had reached the end of its development as far as the increasingly competitive World Superbike Championship was concerned.

Honda still had the exotic works RVF750 race bikes – similar in basic design to the RC30, but representing development work worth millions of dollars. But now the World Endurance series and the Isle of Man TT were to be held under Superbike rules, and the RVF would no longer be eligible.

Honda's answer was to base a new road bike on the RVF, specifically built to win at World Superbike level. Like the RC30, it would be a no-expense-spared, limited production model, and race kits would be available from day one.

It was called the RVF750R, but it's known everywhere by its factory code name – the RC45.

Superficially, it was clearly closely related to the RC30, with its twin spar alloy frame, V-four engine, single-sided swing arm – even a similar paint scheme. But not a single part is interchangeable between the two.

Superbike rules allow scope for changing engine internals, suspension parts, exhausts and wheels, but they don't allow a complete change of fuel system. This was one of the main reasons the RC30 lost its competitive edge – its carburettors were simply no longer up to the job. With the RC45, Honda took the plunge and fitted an electronic fuel injection system. In terms of pure peak power there's probably little advantage in an injection system, but it simplifies the job of altering the fuelling characteristics to suit different atmospheric conditions or engine set-ups. Instead of dismantling a bank of carburettors to change the jets (notoriously difficult with a complex engine layout like the RC's), all a mechanic has to do is alter the settings on an easily-accessible control box.

Racers and road riders alike queued up to place their orders for the new bike – after all, the RC30 had been superb, so what would its replacement be like? Some road riders, in particular, were disappointed. On the road, the RC45 has no real advantage over the RC30. This is partly because the RC30 had already set such high standards: although the RC45 is faster, has better brakes and suspension and more low-down power, there simply isn't anywhere that an average rider can exploit its advantages. The RC45 operates on a plane of efficiency that doesn't mesh very well with speed limits, blind corners and traffic travelling 100mph slower then the RC45 wants to go.

On the race track, too, the RC45 took a while to come good. It was quickly on the pace and running near the front in Superbikes, and was often fastest through the speed traps, but never seemed to translate that into a winning performance. The Ducati 916 had a weight advantage over the Honda

which gave it better acceleration out of corners. The ZXR750 Kawasaki had the benefit of several years' continuous development. The Honda had a handling problem – lack of traction out of corners. It was eventually traced to the rear suspension linkage, which was quickly revised. Soon the RC45 started to notch up race success, with victory in the prestigious Suzuka Eight Hour race and its first World Superbike success in the hands of Aaron Slight at Albacete in Spain. The RC had already proved its reliability with two victories at the Le Mans 24-hour race, and had taken over from the factory RVF as king of the Mountain Course at the Isle of Man. But, two seasons into its Superbike career, it still can't match those damn Ducatis.

Despite persistent problems on the race track, RC45 handling is utterly beyond reproach on the road.

SPECIFICATION: HONDA RC45	
ENGINE	Water-cooled DOHC 16-valve, 90° V-four
DISPLACEMENT	749cc
HORSEPOWER	118bhp @ 12,000rpm
CARBURETTORS	PGM FI fuel injection
GEAR BOX	Six speed
FRAME	Aluminium twin spar
WHEELBASE	55.5ins
WEIGHT	417lbs dry
TOP SPEED	165mph

Kawasaki 1100 Zephyr

Kawasaki were the first Japanese company to look back on their own history for inspiration when designing new bikes. The result was the Zephyr range, introduced in 1991. The 550 and 750 Zephyrs, both styled like Kawasaki's muscle bikes of the 'seventies, sold well to people who were attracted to the simplicity and spirit of a 'seventies bike, but who wanted 'nineties reliability and a warranty. The 'retro' movement was born. But what real muscle bike fans wanted was the true successor to the hairy-chested Z1 and the later Z1000.

They got it in 1992, with the Zephyr 1100.

In stark contrast to the firm's other flagship 1100, the ZZ-R, the Zephyr is a model of simplicity, consisting of little more than an engine, two wheels and just enough other equipment to hold them together. Visually, the Zephyr takes its styling cues from the Z1. But not a standard Z1. What Kawasaki did was to build a bike that incorporated all the modifications people made to their old Zeds as technology moved on and parts from later bikes became available.

So, the Zephyr has an alloy box-section swinging arm at the rear, operating remote reservoir twin shocks with adjustable damping. At the front, huge twin brake discs and four-piston calipers from the ZZ-R1100 are a far cry from the Z1's single front disc and single-piston caliper. Alloy wheels fitted with wide, sticky tyres complete the picture.

The result of all this attention to the running gear is a bike that's superbly balanced, with plenty of ground clearance for fast back-road riding, and impeccable low-speed manners. The Zephyr is a

Kawasaki were the first to exploit the Retro concept, and after-market suppliers have been happy to leap into the same niche. The Cyclone reflects a growing trend towards customised variants.

Tracing its mechanical ancestry all the way back over 20 years to the Z1, the biggest Zephyr's handling is not for the faint-hearted.

heavy bike, but it carries its weight low, making for good manoeuvrability The low seat and upright riding position help here, too – a relief for many after the race crouch of most modern sports bikes.

But it's the engine that gives the Zephyr its real character. The air-cooled unit is based on the old GPz1100 – strong, almost over-engineered, and still a favourite with drag racers and tuners. Freed from the need to produce awesome peak power figures for maximum speed, the engine designers were able to concentrate on getting smooth, strong, useable power from as little as 2,000rpm all the way up to the relatively lowly 9,500rpm red line.

The only concession to the technological advances made since the 'seventies is the air-cooled motor's twin plug set-up. The use of two spark plugs per cylinder helps improve combustion efficiency and beefs up an already fearsome midrange power curve – there are few bikes that give the same impression of arm-tugging acceleration as an 1100 Zephyr. In the real world, the Zephyr's power characteristics make it easy to drive off the line fast, or power hard out of turns without worrying what gear you're in.

If the midrange is impressive, the Zephyr's high speed manners are less so. Flat out at around 140mph, the combination of old-tech chassis and

suspension components, and a riding position that turns you into a sail, means the Zephyr weaves and wobbles along seemingly on the very edge of control. Unless you want to lie flat on the tank, 130mph is a more realistic top speed, and the lack of a fairing means anything over 90mph is uncomfortable for long distances.

But paradoxically, it's this very aspect that makes the Zephyr so popular. Not everyone wants a bike that can do 170mph and handles so well you have to be a budding racer to take it to its limits. There's definitely a place for the Zephyr's low tech, low cost, high fun factor approach, as Honda, Suzuki and Yamaha have since proved by following Kawasaki's lead and producing their own contributions to the retro revolution.

'There are few bikes that give the same impression of arm-tugging acceleration as an 1100 Zephyr.'

SPECIFICATION: KAWASAKI 1100 ZEPHYR	
ENGINE	Air-cooled DOHC 8-valve in-line four
DISPLACEMENT	1062cc
HORSEPOWER	91bhp @ 7900rpm
CARBURETTORS	4 x 34mm Keihin
GEAR BOX	Five speed
FRAME	Tubular steel double cradle
WHEELBASE	59.1in
WEIGHT	534lbs dry
TOP SPEED	140mph

Kawasaki ZX-9R

....

'Accelerating effortlessly from a standstill up to an indicated 170mph without pausing for breath.'

Almost as fast as the awesome ZZ-R1100, the ZX-9R packs a ferocious punch into a far more compact package.

Kawasaki have long been known as manufacturers of superlative superbikes. From the days of the Z1, through the 900 Ninja, to the ZZ-R1100, they have built an enviable reputation for building ultimate in-line fours. Rather than expending time and money on innovation for its own sake and technological dead-ends, the Big 'K' has stuck to what it knows, and perfected it. They have taken the water-cooled DOHC 16-valve in-line four and made it their own.

In recent years Kawasaki have concentrated their efforts in the superbike market on large capacity sports-tourers such as the ZZ-R1100, with the ZXR750 presenting the pinnacle of supersports development in their range. But with the advent of Honda's all-conquering Fireblade, Kawasaki had to produce a fire-breathing 900cc race-replica of their own. The ZX-9R is it, although this is a street racer with a difference.

Rather than produce a bike that featured state-of-the-art handling and race-track performance, Kawasaki attempted to bridge the gap between race-replica and sports-tourer, to produce a bike that had the looks and speed of a race-replica, but which was comfortable for two-up road-riding. They reasoned that some motorcyclists want the style and image of a race-replica, but the comfort and practicality of a more traditional road bike.

To achieve this Kawasaki made it just a little bit bigger and heavier than a mere Kawasaki 'Fireblade'. Without the need to save weight wherever possible they could concentrate on building a superbike that looked suitably aggressive but which was big enough and comfortable enough to satisfy the demands of the man in the street.

Lashings of extra mid-range power makes the 9R easier to ride than the ZXR750, yet it is almost as nimble as its smaller stablemate.

But that doesn't mean the ZX-9R isn't a fine sportsbike in its own right. With a water-cooled DOHC 16-valve in-line four cylinder engine pumping out 125bhp, and a lightweight but strong aluminium-alloy beam frame, the ZX-9R is a performance superbike capable of exceeding 165mph. Multi-adjustable inverted telescopic front forks and a rising-rate rear monoshock give the ZX-9R up-to-the-minute suspension technology and ensure that the handling is as impressive as the engine performance.

Weighing in at 475lbs dry the ZX-9R is no lightweight (it's 70lbs heavier than a Honda CBR900 Fireblade), but that doesn't count against it anywhere except on a race track. On the road the ZX-9R is lightning-quick, blessed with masses of mid-range power and a top-end delivery that takes your breath away. Accelerating effortlessly from a standstill up to an indicated 170mph without pausing for breath, the ZX-9R is the kind of bike that will cover distances quickly, comfortably and with the minimum of fuss. Not quite as quickly and effortlessly as a ZZ-R1100, but not far off, and with the styling and looks of a bike that belongs on a race track.

SPECIFICATION: KAWASAKI ZX-9R	
ENGINE	Water-cooled DOHC 16-valve in-line four
DISPLACEMENT	899cc
HORSEPOWER	125bhp @ 10,500rpm
CARBURETTORS	4 x 40mm Keihin
GEAR BOX	6 speed
FRAME	Aluminium-alloy twin beam
WHEELBASE	56.7ins
WEIGHT	475lbs dry
TOP SPEED	167mph

Kawasaki ZX-7R

....

'It accelerates with a restrained but still spine-tingling growl from the large exhaust can.'

The ZX-7R is the impressive result of several years of relentless development work by Kawasaki. The ZX-7R's predecessor was the ZXR750: a raw, four-cylinder race-replica that was gradually turned into a rapid and refined roadburner in the years following its launch in 1989. When the ZX-7R appeared in 1996, it carried the process of improvement several steps further – without losing the sense of sheer excitement that characterised the ZXR.

The ZX-7R's basic format is identical to that of the ZXR, not to mention several rivals in the competitive 750cc sports bike class. Its water-cooled, 16-valve four-cylinder engine sits in a twin-beam aluminium frame. Its bodywork is sleek and all-enveloping; its riding position stretched-out; its attitude uncompromisingly aggressive.

That was certainly true of the ZXR750, which retained its distinctive character while being updated many times throughout the '90s. Its engine first received more midrange power, then more top-end thanks to the adoption of a ram-air intake system. Its chassis gained frame and brake modifications, and most importantly improved suspension.

The ZX-7R has a new name and a new look, thanks to bold one-colour bodywork in place of the ZXR's contrasting shades, but essentially the new bike is a further development of the same theme. Kawasaki claim its frame is 30 per cent stiffer, thanks to thicker main rails and a larger steering head area. The 43mm front forks are thicker, have polished stanchions to reduce friction and, like the new rear shock, are fully adjustable for the first time.

Numerous engine changes include the adoption of 'short-stroke' dimensions, allowing higher revs. The ram-air system is revised to allow more air in

Kawasaki's 750cc race-replicas have been notable for their aggressive good looks ever since the original ZXR750 of 1989, and the ZX-7R upholds the tradition. Ram-air intakes are clearly visible to each side of the twin headlamp lenses.

via the large ducts alongside the ZX-7R's twin headlamps. New valvegear and a modified four-into-one exhaust system help increase midrange power, although the official maximum output is unchanged at 120bhp. Features such as a bigger radiator and revised cooling system help keep the engine in one piece.

More power or not, the Kawasaki certainly feels mighty fast as the revs climb and it accelerates with a restrained but still spine-tingling growl from the large exhaust can. Although it's a refined machine, the ZX-7R retains the ZXR engine's slightly harsh feel as it heads for the 12,500rpm redline. With a top speed of over 160mph, the ZX is a match for any 750cc four in a straight line.

For rapid riding the ZX-7R's only real drawback is its weight. At 440lbs dry the Kawasaki is fully

35lbs heavier than Honda's more powerful CBR900RR or Suzuki's GSX-R750. Compared to the GSX-R, in particular, the ZX-7R is rather heavy and slow-steering, meaning its rider has to work harder when the pace hots up on a twisty road.

The chassis works well, though, its modifications combining to make this the fastest and best-handling 750cc Kawasaki yet. The ZX is supremely stable, yet turns into corners easily with a light, neutral feel. Its sophisticated suspension soaks up bumps that would have punished a ZXR rider's kidneys, and the six-piston Tokico brake calipers combine with big 320mm discs to give fearsome stopping power.

The ZX-7R might struggle against lighter rivals on a racetrack, but as a roadbike it is up there with the best. Its clean looks, extra midrange power and added chassis sophistication make this the best 750cc Kawasaki yet. And the way in which the ZX-7R blends its raw feel with its new-found refinement ensures a hugely entertaining ride.

Although it's heavier than many rivals, the ZX-7R goes round corners as well as the best of them. Its neutral steering, excellent suspension and fat, grippy tyres make this the best-handling 750cc Kawasaki yet.

In typical Kawasaki style the ZX-7R emits a slightly harsh feel and an evocative exhaust note as the powerful 16-valve engine spins towards its redline — which is set at a heady 12,500rpm.

SPECIFICATION: KAWASAKI ZX-7R	
ENGINE	Water-cooled DOHC 16-valve in-line four
DISPLACEMENT	748cc
HORSEPOWER	120bhp @ 11,800rpm
CARBURETTORS	4 x 38mm Keihin
GEAR BOX	Six speed
FRAME	Aluminium alloy beam
WHEELBASE	55.9ins
WEIGHT	440lbs dry
TOP SPEED	163mph

Kawasaki ZZ-R1100

The Kawasaki ZZ-R1100 is one of the ultimates in the superbikes world. Hugely powerful, stunningly fast and very sleek, the ZZ-R1100 brings eye-watering performance to the mass-market.

Capable of out-performing just about any car on the roads (even the like of Ferarris and Porsches), the ZZ-R1100 costs less than the price of a family saloon. With a top-speed nudging 180mph and a 0-60mph time of less than three seconds, the ZZ-R1100 is a true king of the roads.

So what is surprising about the ZZ-R1100 is how ordinary it really is. It doesn't rely on complicated suspension systems, fancy fuel-injection or curiously-shaped pistons. No, the ZZ-R1100 uses solid, well-proven engine technology and state-of-the-art aerodynamics to produce one of the most impressive superbikes ever seen.

The heart of the ZZ-R1100 is its water-cooled, double overhead cam, 16-valve, in-line four-cylinder engine. Power output varies from country to country according to local laws, but in unrestricted form the ZZ-R1100 makes a whopping 147bhp at 11,000rpm. With a dry weight of 514lbs, that gives the ZZ-R1100 a power-to-weight ratio five times higher than a *very* fast car. One hundred and eighty miles per hour and a standing quarter of a mile in under 11 seconds is territory normally reserved for Italian supercars, but the ZZ-R1100 makes it available to the man in the street!

And what of the rest of the ZZ-R1100? The svelte bodywork is a major contributor to the awesome top speed and it also helps to keep the wind and rain away from the rider. Suspension is handled by a hefty pair of 43mm multi-adjustable telescopic forks at the front and a rising-rate, multi-adjustable monoshock at the back. Twin 320mm front discs seized by four-piston calipers give the ZZ-R much-needed stopping power, with a single 250mm rear disc gripped by a twin-piston caliper to complete the set-up.

The ZZ-R1100 isn't a pure sportsbike, nor was it ever intended to be. Kawasaki have eschewed the race-replica route for their litre bikes, preferring instead to make them potent all-rounders. As a

More 'super' than most, the ZZ-R1100 is the fastest production motorcycle ever built, capable of humbling cars costing ten times the price.

Although not so nimble as Honda's Fireblade, the big 'Kwacker' scratches better than anything *this* big has a right to do.

'The ZZ-R1100 brings eye-watering performance to the mass-market.'

result the ZZ-R1100 is an excellent two-up sports-tourer capable of covering long distances quickly and easily. A large fuel tank and reasonably frugal consumption make the ZZ-R a good long-distance machine, and the rider and pillion accommodation are appropriately comfortable.

There aren't many superbikes with the all-round capabilities of the ZZ-R1100. On the one hand it is a fast, sure-footed sportsbike capable of delivering exceptional performance at the twist of the wrist, while on the other hand it will carry two people a long way in reasonable comfort and with the minimum of fuss. Small wonder, then, that Kawasaki sell so many of them.

Whether it's tricks you want (left), or 1000 touring miles in a day, the ZZ-R1100 effortlessly delivers.

SPECIFICATION: KAWASAKI ZZ-R1100	
ENGINE	Liquid-cooled DOHC 16-valve in-line four
DISPLACEMENT	1052cc
HORSEPOWER	147bhp @ 11000rpm
CARBURETTORS	4 x 40mm Keihin CV
GEAR BOX	Six speed
FRAME	Aluminium-alloy twin beam
WHEELBASE	58.8ins
WEIGHT	514lbs dry
TOP SPEED	175mph

Magni Australia

·····························

'It was on a twisty road, though, that the Australia came into its own.'

A red-and-silver tribute to countless MV *Grand Prix* winners, but the transverse V-twin is every inch a Moto Guzzi – with added Magni class.

Its sleek styling, big V-twin engine and enormous rear tyre showed that this was a serious sports bike, but it was the red-and-silver paintwork that revealed most about the Magni Australia. Those were the colours of the legendary MV Agusta race team once run by Arturo Magni, the Australia's creator.

Magni had prepared the 'Gallarate Fire Engines' raced to glory by John Surtees, Mike Hailwood and Giacomo Agostini. Then, when MV stopped racing after winning 17 consecutive 500cc world titles between 1958 and 1974, Magni set up business with his son Giovanni to build high-quality roadsters from a workshop near Agusta's old base at Gallarate, north of Milan. Several used engines from Moto Guzzi, notably the 1990-model Sfida, a

retro-styled sportster powered by the two-valves-per-cylinder engine from the Le Mans.

Two years later came the fastest and best Magni yet: the Australia, so-called because it was a direct descendent of a Guzzi-engined Magni racebike that had notched up a string of impressive results Down Under. The Australia was powered by the V-twin engine from the Daytona 1000, Guzzi's fuel-injected, eight-valve flagship. To ease homologation the 992cc 'high cam' unit was retained in its entirety from airbox to silencers.

Almost everything else was new, though, most notably the frame. In place of the Daytona's large-diameter spine was a more conventional arrangement, based on three 34mm diameter chrome-molybdenum steel tubes running back

Unlike more commonplace Guzzis, the Australia's steering is light and precise, a tribute to the exceptional quality of its chassis and suspension.

from the steering head. A pair of front downtubes helped secure the engine.

The swing-arm was a single-shock version of Magni's proven Parallelogramo design, created to combat torque-reaction. Rear suspension was provided by a single shock from Dutch firm White Power. The Australia's swing-arm was wide enough to allow fitment of a wide, 180-section rear tyre.

At the front were upside-down Forcelle Italia forks – adjustable, like the shock, for both compression and rebound damping. The 17-inch wheels held 320mm Brembo brake discs with four-piston calipers. Both mudguards were lightweight carbon fibre, helping to keep weight to a respectable 450lb dry.

The cylinder heads visible at each side of the Australia made the Guzzi connection clear, and there was no doubting the engine's origins when it fired up to send the bike rocking in characteristic fashion with every blip of the throttle. At most engine speeds the Australia had a wonderfully loose, rev-happy feel, aided by the Weber-Marelli fuel-injection's crisp response.

With a peak output of 95bhp, the slippery Australia had a top speed of about 140mph, plus generous acceleration from low revs. The Magni pulled strongly almost from tickover, with a slight surge at around 4000rpm that sent it charging along

with a rustling from the aircooled engine's sticking-out cylinders, and a typically long-legged Guzzi feel at high speed.

It was on a twisty road, though, that the Australia came into its own. Its Brembo brakes were superbly powerful, steering was light and the Magni could be cornered easily and with great precision. Suspension was compliant but very well-controlled at both ends, and the drive shaft barely noticeable.

That blend of good looks, effortless engine performance and nimble handling made the Australia a very impressive special, with a captivating blend of pace and grace. Its price was high – but not excessively so for a machine hand-built in tiny numbers. Especially when those hands had once built bikes for legends such as Surtees, Hailwood and Agostini.

Fuel injection helps give the big Guzzi motor impressive responsiveness and punch throughout the rev range, with an un-Guzzi-like eagerness to rev.

SPECIFICATION: MAGNI AUSTRALIA	
ENGINE	Air-cooled high-cam 8-valve 90-degree transverse V-twin
DISPLACEMENT	992cc
HORSEPOWER	95bhp
CARBURETTORS	Weber-Marelli fuel-injection
GEAR BOX	Five speed
FRAME	Tubular steel
WHEELBASE	58ins
WEIGHT	450lbs dry
TOP SPEED	140mph

Moto Guzzi Centauro

'Suddenly, the big V-twin hits its sweet spot and the Centauro comes alive.'

With its bulbous bodywork and Moto Guzzi's familiar transverse V-twin engine, the Centauro is a striking bike that rarely fails to make an impact. Even those who dislike its looks can't deny that it's different.

With its blend of bold, streetwise styling and traditional transverse V-twin engine, the V10 Centauro is rolling proof of Moto Guzzi's re-emergence as a motorcycling force. For years the famous old Italian firm suffered from lack of ideas and investment. But in 1996, under fresh management and making a profit once again, Guzzi confirmed its revitalisation with a striking new model.

The Centauro, whose name comes from the centaur, a half-man, half-horse of Greek mythology, is a naked V-twin with a distinctly aggressive personality. This radically styled bike may have no fairing, but its heart is the 992cc, eight-valve V-twin motor from Guzzi's Daytona flagship – detuned slightly with a softer camshaft but still producing an impressive 90bhp at 8200rpm.

The Centauro's chassis, too, is borrowed from its sportier siblings. The roadster's familiar rectangular-section steel spine frame is identical to that of the 1100 Sport, and the same is almost true of the suspension. Dutch specialist WP's 40mm upside-down forks and rear shock are simply retuned slightly to suit the unfaired V10.

Thanks to the Centauro's flat, large-diameter handlebars and forward-set footrests, there's a distinct feel of Harley-Davidson as you settle into the low, broad seat. But this rumbling, aircooled V-twin motor's torque-reaction roll from side to side when it fires up confirms its origins at Guzzi's base in Mandello del Lario, rather than Milwaukee.

The upright riding position, low seat and generous steering lock combine to make the V10 comfortable and manoeuvrable at slow speed.

Transmission modifications mean it shifts more cleanly and reliably than many previous Guzzis, too, although the five-speed gearbox still requires a deliberate action.

Weber-Marelli's fuel-injection system, a remapped version of the Daytona set-up, gives a crisp low-rev response. There are no flat-spots, and the big V-twin pulls cleanly even when its throttle is cracked open at only 2000rpm in top gear. But although the V10 chugs forward obediently, its low-rev power pulses quickly smoothing out in typical Guzzi style, the bike doesn't stretch its rider's arms through the lower midrange in quite the way that might be expected of an unfaired big-bore twin.

The reason for that becomes clear when the white-faced tachometer's needle reaches 4500rpm: this motor is still very much a rev-happy sportster powerplant. Suddenly, the big V-twin hits its sweet spot and the Centauro comes alive. The surge of acceleration, made even more vivid by the wind tearing at the rider's chest, transforms the docile Centauro into a stampeding stallion.

An indicated 120mph arrives rapidly and with considerably more to come, though you would need a strong neck and arms to hold high speeds for long. Top speed is 135mph, but more importantly the Centauro cruises at 80mph with a typically relaxed Guzzi feel.

Stability at speed is excellent, with no sign of the wobbles that afflict many unfaired bikes. Steering is neutral although at 451lbs the V10 is no lightweight, and quick direction changes require a firm tug on the bars. The well-damped suspension, grippy Pirelli tyres and powerful Brembo brakes give this Guzzi enough cornering performance to show up more than a few race-replicas.

Ultimately much of the Centauro's appeal – or otherwise – comes down to your opinion of its unmistakable looks. For those who appreciate its style, the V10 works well as a distinctive unfaired roadster with the performance of a sports bike. Either way, it's proof that rejuvenated Moto Guzzi is heading for an exciting future.

The Centauro's eight-valve V-twin engine produces more power at high revs than in the midrange. Handling is typically Moto Guzzi: slow-steering but very stable at speed.

Despite its unusual styling the Centauro looks very much like a Guzzi, thanks to the way the big aircooled cylinders of its transverse V-twin engine stick out to each side.

SPECIFICATION: MOTO GUZZI V10 CENTAURO	
ENGINE	Air-cooled SOHC 8-valve V-twin
DISPLACEMENT	992cc
HORSEPOWER	90bhp @ 8200rpm
CARBURETTORS	Weber fuel-injection
GEAR BOX	Five speed
FRAME	Steel spine
WHEELBASE	58.1ins
WEIGHT	451lbs dry
TOP SPEED	135mph

Moto Guzzi 1100 Sport Injection

Few superbikes combine old-fashioned charm and modern technology to such good effect as Moto Guzzi's 1100 Sport Injection. The Italian firm's original 1100 Sport model, launched in 1994, was a handsome and charismatic roadburner, powered by an enlarged version of the traditional aircooled, transverse V-twin engine that Guzzi have been building for decades.

That first Sport model was respectably rapid and very stable, but in comparison with Guzzi's own fuel-injected Daytona (let alone almost every rival firm's sportsters) it was a little rough round the edges. Two years later, Guzzi revamped the big V-twin with fuel-injection and a host of chassis changes – and the result was a resounding success.

Unlike the eight-valve motor of Guzzi's Daytona flagship, the Sport Injection motor has only two valves per cylinder, operated by old-fashioned pushrods. But in place of the old Sport model's carburettors, the 1064cc unit has a Weber fuel-injection system similar to that of the Daytona. Other changes include reshaped gearbox teeth and a new cush-drive in the rear wheel.

The Injection uses a slightly revised version of the old Sport's steel spine frame, a new swing-arm constructed from elliptical-section steel tubes, and a multi-adjustable WP shock. The same Dutch firm also supplies the front forks, 40mm upside-down units with adjustable damping. Brakes are by Brembo, as before, uprated to semi-floating 320mm discs with four piston calipers up front.

The Injection's list of modifications does nothing to alter the basic Guzzi feel, which makes itself known the moment the 90-degree transverse V-twin fires-up to send the bike rocking from side to side. Nor do the engine-related changes increase

The 1100 Sport Injection is visually very similar to its predecessor, the 1100 Sport – but the adoption of fuel-injection and numerous other changes improve the big V-twin's throttle response and give it a more refined feel, without losing the Guzzi's traditional long-legged character.

'Once into its midrange stride the Guzzi really begins to pull hard.'

The Sport Injection's Weber-Marelli fuel system doesn't alter the 1064cc V-twin's 90bhp peak output, but the injected bike has a smoother throttle action and a crisper low-rev response than its predecessor.

the Sport's peak power output of 90bhp at 7800rpm. But they certainly make the bike nicer to ride.

The Guzzi pulls away with noticeably less of a transmission clunk than its predecessor. And the fuel-injected bike's throttle action is both light and quick-action – something that was never possible with the original Sport's 40mm Dell'Orto carburettors.

Best of all, though, is the injected bike's behaviour when the throttle is wrenched open at low revs. Even from well below 3000rpm in top gear, the Sport Injection responds crisply, its motor juddering slightly but sending the bike rumbling instantly forward when its carburetted predecessor would just have coughed and spluttered in protest.

Once into its midrange stride the Guzzi really begins to pull hard, accelerating with an effortless feel typical of the marque when it reaches its sweet zone between 5000 and 7000rpm. The old pushrod unit gets a bit breathless and rough after that, and there is little point in taking it to the 8000rpm redline. But given enough room the Injection will rumble up to a top speed of about 140mph.

Handling is good, too, despite the Injection's substantial 486lbs of weight. Guzzis are traditionally very stable, and this one is no exception. The bike steers slowly by modern sports bike standards, but it is still flickable enough to be fun on a twisty road. And although the Injection's Pirelli Dragons are not

the widest of superbike tyres, they certainly give plenty of grip.

The Sport Injection's excellent throttle response and reliable handling make this a very easy machine to ride fast. Along with the old Sport model's retained good looks and V-twin character, the result is a bike that excels at the things Moto Guzzis traditionally do well, and has far fewer of the old faults. No wonder many enthusiasts consider it quite simply the best big Guzzi yet.

SPECIFICATION: MOTO GUZZI 1100 SPORT INJECTION	
ENGINE	Air-cooled OHV 4-valve 90-degree transverse V-twin
DISPLACEMENT	1064cc
HORSEPOWER	90bhp @ 7800rpm
CARBURETTORS	Weber fuel-injection
GEAR BOX	Five speed
FRAME	Tubular steel spine
WHEELBASE	58ins
WEIGHT	486lbs dry
TOP SPEED	140mph

Like any big Guzzi, the Sport Injection steers slowly by modern superbike standards. But its suspension is good and it's stable in corners.

Suzuki GSX-R750

··············

W hen Suzuki unveiled the long-awaited successor to its GSX-R750 sportster in 1996, few people believed that the new bike could make the same sort of impact as its predecessor. After all, the original GSX-R750, introduced 11 years earlier, had become a legend. Powerful, outrageously light and stunningly fast, it had annihilated all opposition and sparked the cult of the aluminium-framed Japanese race-replica.

Those doubters reckoned without Suzuki's peerless ability to build singleminded high-performance motorcycles. Sure enough, with the new-generation GSX-R, Suzuki has managed to create a machine with precisely the original model's no-compromise approach. It's arguably the leanest, fiercest, most gloriously irresponsible vehicle on two wheels.

Statistics don't come close to telling the whole story, but they are revealing all the same. The GSX-R750's peak power output of 126bhp matches that of Honda's mighty CBR900RR Fireblade and exceeds all other 750s. The Suzuki weighs just 394lbs, making it lighter than most *600cc* fours. It has the same steering geometry and wheelbase as the Suzuki RGV500 grand prix bike ridden to the 1993 world championship by Kevin Schwantz.

Although the GSX-R's approach is unchanged, it shares very few components with its predecessor. The engine's dramatically increased power output and reduced size and weight required some major modifications, notably the adoption of a ram-air intake system. Internal changes to the 16-valve, watercooled engine include more oversquare cylinder dimensions, the camchain moved to the end of the crankshaft, cylinders set closer together, and many other parts made smaller and lighter.

The frame is a conventional twin-beam aluminium construction, in contrast to the old GSX-R's taller and less rigid aluminium cradle. Despite its neat styling and distinctive, swoopy tail-piece, this makes the Suzuki look slightly ordinary – but any notion that this is just another Japanese in-line four changes the second you ride it. Even at a standstill the GSX-R feels outrageously light and manoeuvrable. Once under way, the ultra-responsive Suzuki flicks into corners almost before its rider realises they've arrived.

Such a short, light, quick-steering bike can't help being a bit frisky when accelerating hard, and on a bumpy road the GSX-R can be a real handful. The original GSX-R750 pushed frame, suspension and tyre technology to the limit, resulting in occasional tank-slappers, and the current model inherits the family trait.

But in most situations the handling is superb, thanks to the frame's rigidity and the control provided by sophisticated, multi-adjustable upside-down forks and monoshock. Fat, sticky radial tyres make good use of the generous ground clearance. And the front brake combination of twin 320mm

The modern GSX-R750 is a much more compact and streamlined machine than its famous forebear from 1985, but the two bikes have much in common — notably mind-blowing acceleration at high revs, ultra-light weight and a tendency to feel twitchy at speed.

discs gripped by six-piston calipers, although rather wooden in town, is phenomenally powerful at speed.

Inevitably the GSX-R thrives on revs, requiring frequent tune-playing with the slick six-speed gearbox to give of its best. Keep the tacho needle flicking towards the redline at a heady 13,500rpm, and the Suzuki provides searing acceleration towards a top speed of 165mph. Although there is nothing like as much power available lower down, for such a highly-strung machine the GSX-R is reasonably tractable.

Naturally, a bike as singleminded as this has its drawbacks. The GSX-R is cramped and firmly suspended, it requires too much rider input ever to

be remotely relaxing, and its low screen gives little wind protection. But when you ride the Suzuki on the right road, none of those things matters at all. It's super-fast, supremely agile and absolutely crazy – every bit a true GSX-R750.

This GSX-R's most distinctive feature is its exaggerated seat hump, which combines with the low, swept-back screen to give smooth air-flow for maximum straight-line performance.

Few other superbikes come even close to matching the GSX-R's superbly light and precise steering feel, but inevitably the drawback is marginal stability.

SPECIFICATION: SUZUKI GSX-R750	
ENGINE	Water-cooled DOHC 16-valve in-line four
DISPLACEMENT	749cc
HORSEPOWER	126bhp @ 12,000rpm
CARBURETTORS	Four 39mm Mikuni
GEAR BOX	Six speed
FRAME	Aluminium alloy beam
WHEELBASE	55.1ins
WEIGHT	394lbs dry
TOP SPEED	165mph

'The Suzuki provides searing acceleration.'

Suzuki GSF 1200 Bandit

Due to its slightly raised handlebars and lack of a fairing, Suzuki's GSF1200 Bandit is commonly referred to as a retro-bike – and in one sense that's just what it is. The Bandit brings to mind Suzuki's GSX1100, a bike which, back in the early '80s before the Japanese manufacturers discovered fairings, was perhaps the best of the powerful, heavy but increasingly well-mannered fours.

Like the old GSX, the Bandit is a naked machine with a 16-valve four-cylinder engine. The modern bike's clean-cut styling is similar to that of its predecessor, too. But that's where relevance of the 'retro' tag ends. Because far from being a softly-tuned piece of nostalgia, the Bandit is a powerful, fine-handling, wheelie-loving and thoroughly modern superbike.

Its engine is based on the oil-cooled unit from the fearsome GSX-R1100 sportster, bored-out by 1mm to 1157cc and detuned slightly to give more midrange torque at the expense of top-end power. Lowered compression ratio plus revised ignition and cam timing reduce peak power output to 98bhp, and allow maximum torque to be produced at just 4500rpm.

If the Bandit's engine is an ideal powerplant for a big naked bike, its chassis is every bit as good. The 1200's tubular steel frame is similar to that of the GSF600 Bandit, strengthened and fitted with a bigger aluminium swing-arm. The 1200's wheelbase is short by the standards of big retro-bikes, its steering geometry is steep, and most importantly the Bandit is light – at 464lbs it weighs less than all its closest rivals.

Suzuki didn't skimp on the Bandit's cycle parts, either. Its forks are sturdy 43mm units with adjustable spring preload and, instead of the old-style pair of rear shocks fitted to most so-called retros, the GSF has a modern monoshock complete with rising-rate linkage. Fat, low-profile tyres and fully-floating brake discs with four-piston calipers complete an impressive picture.

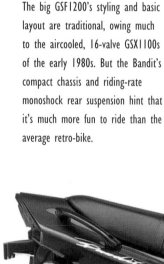

The big GSF1200's styling and basic layout are traditional, owing much to the aircooled, 16-valve GSX1100s of the early 1980s. But the Bandit's compact chassis and riding-rate monoshock rear suspension hint that it's much more fun to ride than the average retro-bike.

Happily the Bandit is every bit as much fun as its spec sheet suggests. The engine is smooth and strong, responding instantly to a crack of the throttle to send the bike hurtling forwards at a thrilling rate. Overall gearing is lower than the GSX-R1100's. Combined with the generous low-rev torque and short wheelbase, this means a Bandit rider requires great self-control to avoid leaving every set of traffic lights with the front wheel in the air . . .

The gutsy motor is equally impressive on the open road, where its crisp midrange power delivery makes for effortless overtaking. Top speed is 140mph, although the naked bike's windblown riding position keeps cruising speed well below three figures. (If that's a problem, the Bandit is also available with a half-fairing.)

Just as the old GSX1100 was generally the best-handling big four back in the early '80s, so the GSF1200 is the pick of the modern naked bikes on a twisty road. Its frame is strong, suspension at both ends is well-controlled, steering is light without being twitchy, and the big twin discs give plenty of stopping power.

The Bandit is even commendably practical for an unfaired bike, although its small fuel tank requires frequent top-ups. The riding position is roomy; the seat is well-padded and big enough for a passenger. And despite the GSF's general air of high quality production, it retails at a remarkably competitive price.

Given all those attributes, it's no surprise that the GSF1200 has become a best seller for Suzuki. Its success is thoroughly deserved. The Bandit is one of those bikes that puts a huge smile on the face of everyone who rides it.

There's nothing special about the Bandit's peak power figure of 98bhp, but cracking open the throttle reveals the 1157cc four's wonderfully strong midrange output. This picture shows the version with half-fairing, which makes for more comfortable high speed cruising.

'The engine is smooth and strong, responding instantly to a crack of the throttle.'

SPECIFICATION: SUZUKI GSF1200 BANDIT	
ENGINE	Oil-cooled DOHC 16-valve in-line four
DISPLACEMENT	1157cc
HORSEPOWER	98bhp @ 5500rpm
CARBURETTORS	Four 36mm Mikuni
GEAR BOX	Five speed
FRAME	Tubular steel duplex cradle
WHEELBASE	56.5ins
WEIGHT	464lbs dry
TOP SPEED	140mph

Suzuki RF900

·····························

When Honda's Fireblade rekindled interest in the 900 class in 1992, the other manufacturers were caught on the hop. For Suzuki the matter was urgent – overnight the Fireblade had usurped both the GSX-R1100's position as the definitive nutter's bike, and the GSX-R750's top spot in the handling stakes. But it had also gained a reputation as a bike which was hard to get the best out of – a real racer on the road. Suzuki saw the gap for a slightly softer-edged machine, easier to use and more practical, but still possessing awesome straight-line performance. The RF900 – styled and badged as a big brother to the existing RF600 – was launched for 1994.

Like the RF600, the 900 was built to a tight budget, developing existing technology rather than starting from scratch with a whole new design.

The water-cooled engine is based on the well-proven GSX-R range, and combines the free-revving nature of the 750 with the low-down pulling power of the 1100. But it's far more than just a sleeved-down 1100 or a big-bore 750. The RF's engine is so well-developed it has a character all of its own. The carburation, in particular, is perfect, allowing the rider to crack the throttle open at any revs and be rewarded with instant performance. Whilst the 900's outright performance doesn't set any records – slightly faster in still conditions than a Fireblade but a long way off the class-leading 170mph+ of the ZX-9, its real strength is in its all-round performance.

'Suzuki saw the gap for a slightly softer-edged machine.'

The surprise package of '94, Suzuki's RF900 exploded onto the scene with blistering performance at a truly amazing bargain price.

The RF's styling, inherited from its RF600 stablemate, isn't to everyone's taste. But as in so many other areas, the RF's policy of getting the job done first and worrying about appearances later pays off. The fairing does an excellent job of directing air around the rider, and the bulbous tail unit carries a seriously wide and comfortable seat with a proper pillion grab rail. The RF is one of the few serious performance bikes that are genuinely comfortable two-up.

Despite pushing it very close in the performance stakes, the steel-framed RF was never meant to compete head-on with the Fireblade, and weighs in around 40lbs heavier than Honda's rocketship. In theory that puts the Suzuki at a serious disadvantage, but in the real world the extra weight gives the RF a comfortable ride, with a feeling of solidity that the pared-down 'Blade can't achieve. It does this with old-tech, but well-matched, suspension components – no fashionable upside-down forks or single-sided swingarms here. But that doesn't mean the RF can't corner hard – it can. The weight distribution's more sporty than touring, and the emphasis is on stability. 120mph sweeping bends are the RF900's favourite stamping grounds, but it tackles everything from backroads to the occasional racetrack with the same easy, do-anything, go-anywhere competence.

For anyone trying an RF900 for the first time, there are two surprises. First, that something apparently styled for long-distance comfort offers such shattering performance and competent, hard-charging handling. Second, that it's cheap – nearly ten per cent cheaper than Suzuki's own GSX-R750. If the Fireblade broke the mould by proving that big bikes didn't need to be bruising heavyweights, the RF did the same by proving that high performance need not cost the Earth.

The RF's prodigious horsepower gleefully shrugs off the limitations of a heavy steel frame and slightly down-market suspension.

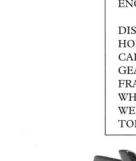

SPECIFICATION: SUZUKI RF900	
ENGINE	Water-cooled DOHC 16-valve in-line four
DISPLACEMENT	937cc
HORSEPOWER	124bhp @ 10,000rpm
CARBURETTORS	4 x 36mm Mikuni
GEAR BOX	Six speed
FRAME	Pressed steel twin spar
WHEELBASE	56.7ins
WEIGHT	447lbs dry
TOP SPEED	165mph

Comparatively restrained styling reflects the 900's role as a high-speed all-rounder rather than a race track escapee.

Suzuki TL1000S

....

'The Suzuki's handling adds to the bike's ultra-sporty, take-no-prisoners attitude.'

With a powerful V-twin engine, a light and innovative chassis and an uncompromisingly aggressive attitude, Suzuki's TL1000S is a stunning machine that heralds a new era for Japanese sports bikes. Suzuki's GSX-R fours have long defined the limits of cutting-edge race-replica design – and the TL follows their example to end Ducati's domination of the V-twin super-sports bike market in emphatic style.

Such was the secrecy with which Suzuki developed the TL that the bike's launch at the Cologne Show in late 1996 shocked not only Ducati but also Honda, whose own VTR1000 V-twin was revealed at the same time. Compared to the rounded VTR, the TL1000S is a no-compromise machine in typical Suzuki mould, complete with fuel-injection, radical steering geometry and even race-compound Metzeler tyres as standard fitment.

Tucked below the strikingly styled Suzuki's half-fairing is a watercooled, 8-valve, 90-degree V-twin engine whose pair of huge 98mm pistons combines with a short 66mm stroke to give a capacity of 996cc. The motor is fed by a ram-air system and uses a specially-developed Mikuni-Denso fuel-injection set-up to help develop impressive horsepower. Peak output is a claimed 123bhp, giving the Suzuki a distinct edge over the 916 and VTR.

The all-new engine is superb, but it's the TL's chassis that reveals Suzuki's engineering at its best. The frame is an aluminium lattice design, developed for visual impact as well as performance, which incorporates a unique rear suspension system consisting of a single spring (placed near-horizontally on the right) and separate rotary damper. This compact arrangement allows the engine to be placed further back, with its rear cylinder where a conventional shock would be, giving a short wheelbase for extra manoeuvrability.

Other cycle parts are conventional and of high quality, notably the multi-adjustable, upside-down Kayaba forks, and the front brake combination of 320mm discs and four-piston Nissin calipers. The TL's dry weight is just 411lbs, and its steering angle is a racy 23.7 degrees – so it's no surprise that the

The TL1000S's half-fairing leaves the big V-twin engine on display, and also reveals the distinctive aluminium frame. Rear suspension is a unique combination of single spring and separate rotary damper.

Suzuki is a thrilling, quick-steering machine that requires its rider to keep totally alert at all times.

That big V-twin motor pulls crisply at low and medium revs, giving enough instant acceleration to lift the front wheel with just a twist of the throttle. And the free-revving engine really takes off at 6500rpm, sending the tacho needle shooting round to the 10,500rpm redline, and hurling the TL forward towards a top speed of 160mph.

The Suzuki's handling adds to the bike's ultra-sporty, take-no-prisoners attitude, as the bike's light weight and radical geometry combine with its awesome acceleration to make the steering very light – sometimes to the point of instability. But if the inevitable drawback of providing effortless steering response and rapid direction changes is twitchiness on a bumpy road, that's a price many riders are willing to pay.

In other respects the TL's chassis is exemplary. Suspension control at both ends is excellent (that unique rotary damper really works), the brakes are powerful and have lots of feel, ground clearance is almost limitless, and the sticky standard-fitment Metzelers complete a package that puts the Suzuki right up there with the world's best and fastest sports bikes of any engine configuration.

Better still, the TL1000S combines its cutting-edge performance and technical sophistication with a very competitive price tag. For riders who always lusted after a rapid V-twin but lack the commitment (financial and otherwise) to own Ducati's demanding 916, the TL1000S provides a challenging and exhilarating alternative.

Motorbikes don't come much more outrageous than the TL1000S, which combines razor-sharp handling with a gloriously free-revving engine. Cracking open the throttle in first or second gear makes the front wheel reach for the sky.

Much of the credit for the TL1000S's crisp throttle response goes to the Mikuni-Denso fuel-injection system.

SPECIFICATION: SUZUKI TL1000S	
ENGINE	Water-cooled DOHC 8-valve 90-degree V-twin
DISPLACEMENT	996cc
HORSEPOWER	123bhp @ 8500rpm
CARBURETTORS	Mikuni-Denso fuel-injection
GEAR BOX	Six speed
FRAME	Aluminium alloy trellis
WHEELBASE	55.7ins
WEIGHT	411lbs dry
TOP SPEED	160mph

Triumph T595 Daytona

....

'It's enough to send the sleek, fully-faired T595 screaming to a top speed of about 165mph.'

There's no mistaking that the T595 Daytona is a pure-bred sports bike, from the tip of its twin-headlamp fairing to the end of its equally streamlined seat unit. Smooth aerodynamics contribute to the Triumph's impressive top speed of over 160mph.

The stylish and super-fast T595 Daytona is the machine that British sports bike enthusiasts dreamt of following Triumph's comeback in 1991. The Hinckley firm's rapid growth since then has been based on its modular format, by which many components are shared between different models. The compromises this involves do not allow a competitive super-sports bike – but in planning the new-generation Daytona, Triumph's engineers had no such constraints and made an all-out attack.

The engine of the T595 (the production bike uses the factory code-name, in the tradition of the old Meriden-based Triumph company) is based on the original watercooled, 12-valve triple. But so much has been changed that it is effectively a completely new motor. Increasing the bore by 3mm to 79mm pushes capacity out to 955cc. New semi-forged pistons ensure that there's no increase in weight.

Lotus Engineering helped tune the motor by allowing it to breathe better. The valves are larger, lighter and reshaped to improve gas flow. Camshaft profile is revised, and the crankshaft and balancer are lightened. Engine weight is further reduced by magnesium covers, modified crankcases and a redesigned gearbox and clutch.

The Daytona's three-into-one exhaust uses stainless steel castings designed for efficient flow, and ends at an oval-section single silencer. A redesigned airbox feeds a sophisticated Sagem fuel-injection and ignition system, whose black box delivers a claimed three million instructions every second.

In place of Triumph's traditional and rather tall steel spine frame is a distinctive perimeter design based around twin oval-section aluminium extrusions. Styling was a key factor in the chassis design, hence the Daytona frame's polished-and-lacquered tubes and the thick single-sided swing-

Handling is superb, the T595's combination of fairly light, neutral steering and confidence-inspiring stability proving just about perfect for rapid road riding. At 436lbs dry the Triumph is slightly heavier than its sportiest rivals, and requires a little more steering effort, but the British bike is correspondingly more stable.

The rather top-heavy feel of previous Triumphs is completely gone, replaced by a pleasantly manageable feel, and backed-up by excellent control from the compliant yet well-controlled suspension from Japanese firm Showa. Brakes, too, are Japanese – and Nissin's front-brake combination of 320mm fully-floating discs and four-piston calipers gives supremely powerful stopping.

However long you examine the T595, and however hard you ride it, there's no doubting that Triumph has really got it right. The new Daytona is every bit as good as it looks. Britain once again has a sporting superbike that stands comparison with the very best in the world.

Although the T595 is designed for fast road riding, with a blend of light steering and high-speed stability, the triple is more than capable of holding its own at high speed on a racetrack.

Triumph's management is happy to admit that styling was regarded as a key element of the T595's design, and the triple combines good looks with high-quality engineering. With its curvaceous bodywork, distinctive oval-section tubular aluminium frame and single-sided rear swing-arm, the Daytona is a stunning bike that heralds an exciting new era for the reborn British manufacturer.

arm. The bike is much more compact than previous Triumphs; its riding position a typical race-replica crouch to fairly wide clip-ons.

The new powerplant is much punchier than its predecessors, kicking super-hard anywhere above 6000rpm to send the bike howling forward urgently and the tacho needle flicking towards the 10,500rpm redline. Peak output is a claimed 128bhp at 10,200rpm, 15bhp up on the old Super Three figure and competitive with the world's best sports bikes. It's enough to send the sleek, fully-faired T595 screaming to a top speed of about 165mph.

Low-rev response is crisp, too, although there is a distinct torque dip at about 5500rpm, which can be frustrating because it's the engine speed at which you quite often find yourself dialling in some extra throttle for overtaking. The Daytona's only other slight disappointment is its rather inconsistent six-speed gearbox – surprising considering previous Triumphs' excellent boxes.

SPECIFICATION: TRIUMPH T595 DAYTONA	
ENGINE	Water-cooled DOHC 12-valve in-line triple
DISPLACEMENT	955cc
HORSEPOWER	128bhp @ 10,200rpm
CARBURETTORS	Sagem fuel-injection
GEAR BOX	Six speed
FRAME	Aluminium alloy tubes
WHEELBASE	56.7ins
WEIGHT	436lbs dry
TOP SPEED	165mph

Triumph T509 Speed Triple

The naked T509 gives a clear view not only of its oval-section aluminium frame – which is identical to that of the T595 apart from its paint finish – but also its 885cc three-cylinder engine, which uses parts from both the old Speed Triple and new T595 powerplants.

Triumph's new-generation Speed Triple roadster, the T509, is one of the most entertaining bikes on the road – as well as one of the most visually striking. With its twin frog-eye headlights up front, and its three-cylinder engine on show to the world, the T509 has a raw, aggressive 'streetfighter' look that many riders love, some dislike but none can fail to notice.

The original Speed Triple was one of Triumph's most popular models worldwide, and its 1997 replacement combines a similar naked musclebike image with many of the components developed for the T595 Daytona. The T509's motor uses a combination of old and new parts, while its chassis is almost identical to that of the T595. The updated Speed Triple might not have a fairing, but in every other respect it's a seriously sporty machine.

Its engine is closer to that of the T595 than the old Speed Triple unit. The original 855cc capacity is retained, as are the cylinder head, pistons and con-rods. But everything else is new, including the aluminium cylinder liners and the lightened crankshaft and clutch. The new Triple's Sagem fuel-injection system is a revised version of that used by the T595, and the airbox and three-into-one exhaust system are also similar. The result is a claimed peak output of 106bhp at 9100rpm, 9bhp up on the old Speed Triple.

The T509's chassis is even closer to that of the T595. This bike's oval-section aluminium frame differs only in that it is painted, instead of polished and lacquered as on the Daytona. The naked Triumph also features identical multi-adjustable 45mm Showa front forks, fully-floating Nissin front brake discs with four-piston calipers, and single-sided swing-arm. All are top-class components of a kind that many unfaired machines make do without.

Differences in engine tune, as well as the lack of a fairing, mean that the T509 is a very different bike to ride to its T595 relation. Rather than delivering its best power at high engine speeds, the Speed Triple is designed to punch out torque in the midrange zone where it's most useful on a naked roadster. Its engine's flexible nature means there's no need for frequent use of the six-speed gearbox – just flick into top and enjoy the ride.

The T509 is most impressive between 3000rpm and about 7000rpm, after which the motor starts to run out of breath as it heads towards the redline at 9500rpm. The Speed Triple will go very fast if you want it to – accelerating hard to a top speed of about 135mph – but on the road it's happiest cruising at up to 120mph. At those speeds the rider gets some wind-protection from the instruments, and the Triumph feels pleasantly smooth and refined.

SPECIFICATION:	TRIUMPH T509 SPEED TRIPLE
ENGINE	Water-cooled DOHC 12-valve in-line triple
DISPLACEMENT	885cc
HORSEPOWER	106bhp @ 9100rpm
CARBURETTORS	Sagem fuel-injection
GEAR BOX	Six speed
FRAME	Aluminium alloy tubes
WHEELBASE	56.7ins
WEIGHT	431lbs dry
TOP SPEED	135mph

Handling, braking and roadholding are every bit as good as might be expected of a bike with such a high-tech chassis. At 431lbs the T509 is light for a big naked machine, and its aluminium frame is supremely rigid. Showa's suspension is firm without being harsh, and very well-damped. Both ends keep control even when the Triumph is putting down lots of torque through its massive and very grippy 190-section rear tyre.

Inevitably the T509's striking styling is the feature that attracts the attention initially, but after riding the Triumph it's the way the bike performs that stays in the mind.

If a lean, muscular roadster with twin headlamps, plenty of torque, a fat back tyre and a thoroughly nasty image appeals to you, then rest assured. The T509 Speed Triple delivers everything it threatens.

For a naked roadster the T509 handles superbly, thanks to its rigid frame, top-quality Showa suspension and broad radial tyres. The Speed Triple makes an impact even when it's parked, with its frog-eye twin headlamps. The optional-extra flyscreen adds the finishing touch to a very distinctive bike.

Triumph Sprint 900

'The quality of paint and plating is as high as anything in motorcycling.'

The 900 Sprint, like the rest of the Triumph range, is part Superbike, part miracle. After the once-mighty British motorcycle industry self-destructed during the '60s and '70s, the prospects of regeneration on anything like its former scale were as likely as an (old-style) Triumph twin that didn't vibrate or leak oil. True, there had been occasional flourishes from the likes of Norton and Matchless, but these were very small scale and, it turned out, ill-fated.

Triumph is different. To date John Bloor, the Midlands builder who owns the new company, has sunk around £80 million into the venture. The Hinckley, Leicestershire factory is as modern and efficient as any in the world. Its state-of-the-art computer-controlled machinery will produce well over 10,000 motorcycles during 1995. And, most important of all, the product is good.

The Sprint is a case in point. It eschews race replica performance, in favour of a formula which simply works. Yet originally it wasn't even Triumph's idea. When the naked Trident range first appeared in 1991, a number of customisers, notably in Britain and Germany, produced a half-faired variant. One year later Triumph themselves responded with the Sprint.

But there was a difference. Where the 'unofficial' Sprints had simply been modified Tridents, the official version was actually more of a defrocked version of the fully-faired Trophy. So from the outset the Sprint had the Trophy's dual-rate front springs and both pre-load and rebound damping adjustment at the rear. Although still too softly sprung for out-and-out sport riding, the latter is a useful bonus, allowing the suspension to be fine-tuned to suit conditions. On maximum damping, there is less of the mild wallow to which the unfaired bike is prone.

The result not only *looks* like a motorcycle ought, but makes for a versatile and practical all-rounder. Highish 'bars and lower seat offer a riding position as relaxed as anything this side of a full-blown tourer (and better then several of those). Once you've become used to wielding the wide 'bars from low behind the bulbous tank, the bike is beguilingly easy to control. The half fairing largely eliminates wind fatigue. For long trips by motorway or fast A-roads, it is almost indispensable.

SPECIFICATION: TRIUMPH SPRINT 900	
ENGINE	Liquid-cooled DOHC 16-valve transverse four
DISPLACEMENT	885cc
HORSEPOWER	100bhp @ 9500rpm
CARBURETTORS	3 x 36mm Mikuni CV
GEAR BOX	Six speed
FRAME	Tubular steel spine
WHEELBASE	58.7ins
WEIGHT	474lbs dry
TOP SPEED	136mph

'Invented' by aftermarket specialists, the 900 Sprint quickly became one of the most successful models in the Triumph range, offering a rare brand of performance and practicality.

As well as the rider, the fairing gives the engine an easier time. 100 horsepower shoving a naked Trident through the air has a much tougher time than the same power pushing a comparatively slippery fairing. As with the 900 Daytona, the simple appliance of a dash of aerodynamics makes an already potent engine seem even stronger.

In just a few short years we have come to expect a high standard of finish from Triumph, and the Sprint does not disappoint. The quality of paint and plating is as high as anything in motorcycling, BMW included. Carburation and clutch action are equally refined, and the gear change is superbly precise.

And the three-cylinder engine, of course, is special: flexible, inexhaustible and strong. It thrives on revs, yet punches hard through the mid-range. Like all its siblings, it employs a balance shaft to reduce vibration, but not at the expense of 'character'. Somehow, something distinctive gets through to the rider. You can't quite put your finger on it, but there's a rumble, a cadence, *something*, which says 'I am not a four, and especially not a Japanese four: I am *different*'.

No concealing race-replica styling here, and the Sprint's superb powerplant certainly has no reason to be bashful.

Triumph Thunderbird

'The Thunderbird's chassis was well up to containing its engine performance.'

Although the T-bird's striking styling slightly compromised its performance, the first Retro Triumph instantly vaulted to the head of Hinckley's sales figures. It now accounts for 30 per cent of total production.

One glance at the Thunderbird said everything about the bike that Triumph created to spearhead its return to the American market in 1995. The three-cylinder cruiser was built for nostalgia, echoing the British firm's 1950s and '60s look from its high bars and chrome headlamp all the way to its wire wheels and old-style 'peashooter' silencers. The name added to the period feel, too, for the original 650cc Thunderbird parallel twin had been a big US hit for Triumph in the '50s, and was the bike famously ridden by Marlon Brando's character, Johnny, in *The Wild One*.

The Thunderbird represented a big step for the fast-expanding Hinckley firm, as it was the first model to move significantly away from the modular concept on which Triumph's range had been based. Although the basic layout of this bike's watercooled, twin-cam, 12-valve powerplant was shared with the eight other triples in the range, numerous engine and chassis components were unique, making the Thunderbird more complicated and expensive to produce.

Triumph retained the big triple's familiar 885cc capacity, but the T-bird's cylinder head, crankcases and covers were restyled to mimic those of old aircooled models. Internal changes, including different cams and a lower compression ratio, reduced peak power to 69bhp from the normal 97bhp. Like the Speed Triple, the new triple also had five, rather than Triumph's more common six ratios in its gearbox.

The frame's main spine was similar to the other models', but joined a modified rear section that allowed a slightly lower dual-seat. Bodywork was all new, and did a great job of recapturing the look of the old twins. The classical 'mouth-organ' tank-badge was almost identical to the '50s original. The fuel tank's shape, the chrome carb-covers and wire-spoked wheels (in 18-inch front, 16-inch rear sizes) all added to the period effect.

Triumph's previous triples had been superbly tractable, yet the detuned engine was even stronger at low revs (peak torque arrives at just 4800rpm). Given a handful of throttle, the Triumph surged forwards almost regardless of how far the tacho needle was from its 8500rpm redline. The motor was wonderfully smooth, too, and the gearbox typically slick. Top-end performance was less impressive, as the T-bird began running out of breath well before its modest top speed of 122mph.

The Thunderbird's chassis was well up to containing its engine performance. The frame was stiff, and suspension at both ends firm by cruiser standards. Hard riding, particularly over a series of bumps, sometimes revealed the handling's limitations with a slight twitch. Unlike other Triumphs, this bike made do with a single front disc brake, but it was effective providing the lever was given a solid squeeze.

For short trips and gentle cruising the Thunderbird was comfortable, manoeuvrable and very pleasant indeed. Inevitably, some practicality had been sacrificed to style. This bike's fuel tank held only 3.3 gallons, compared to the 5.5 gallons of most other Triumphs, limiting range to about 100 miles. By then, the wind-blown riding position had normally made the rider glad of a stop, despite the broad and comfortable dual seat.

Triumph offered extra practicality – and style – with a range of accessories including a screen and panniers. But many riders preferred the added retro image of cosmetic options such as traditional two-tone paintwork and rubber knee-pads for the fuel-tank. That carefully cultivated air of nostalgia, combined with good performance and excellent build quality, rapidly made the new Thunderbird a big hit – not just in America but all over the world.

SPECIFICATION:	TRIUMPH THUNDERBIRD
ENGINE	Water-cooled DOHC
	12-valve in-line triple
DISPLACEMENT	885cc
HORSEPOWER	69bhp @ 8000rpm
CARBURETTORS	3 x 36mm Mikuni
GEAR BOX	Five speed
FRAME	Tubular steel spine
WHEELBASE	61ins
WEIGHT	484lbs dry
TOP SPEED	122mph

The Thunderbird's name, 'mouth organ' tank badge and acres of chrome plate hark back – and forward? – to an age when Triumph motorcycles ruled America.

Triumph Trophy 1200

The first of revitalised Triumph's modular superbikes caused a sensation when it was released in 1991. A big, four-cylinder machine designed to deliver both performance and comfort, the Trophy 1200 was fast, smooth, stable, sophisticated – a match in almost every department for the very best sports-tourers on the roads. So impressive was the British firm's debut model that it could have been built by one of the Japanese giants.

Instead it had been developed from scratch by the team led by John Bloor, the multi-millionaire builder who had bought bankrupt Triumph from the liquidator in 1983. Bloor then spent eight years secretly building an impressive new factory at Hinckley, not far from Triumph's old Meriden base, and planning a range of modular machines. Three- and four-cylinder engine layouts used alternative crankshafts to produce four different motors. These powered six initial models, the biggest of which was the four-cylinder Trophy.

Apart from its modular construction, which was unique in the bike world, the Trophy's 1180cc engine was conventional. The watercooled in-line four contained 16 valves, worked by twin overhead camshafts, and produced a very respectable maximum of 125bhp at 9000rpm. More impressive still was its crisp carburation and outstanding supply of midrange torque, which made riding the big Triumph delightfully easy and relaxing.

Instant acceleration was available everywhere, from below 2000rpm to the redline at 9500rpm. Simply winding back the throttle sent the Trophy hurtling forward with a breathtaking mixture of power, tractability and smoothness. There were no power steps, just a steady stream of irrepressible torque that sent the Triumph surging towards a top-speed of just over 150mph and made its excellent six-speed gearbox almost redundant. Better still, efficient twin balancer shafts ensured that vibration was minimal at all engine speeds.

Triumph's modular approach was also employed in the chassis, notably the frame, shared

Arguably the most effortless powerplant in motorcycling, the Trophy's is precisely 1¹/₃ Triumph triples. The extra cylinder gives lashings of additional torque to what was already a potent engine.

Trophy design has evolved to make it a high-speed mile-eater with few equals . . .

. . . yet it can still do this (left) with startling panache.

by all six models and based around a single large-diameter steel spine that incorporated the engine as a stressed member. The frame held 43mm forks and a vertical rear monoshock, both from Japanese specialists Kayaba. Brakes were also made in Japan, by Nissin. Twin-piston front calipers squeezed a pair of 296mm discs up front, giving braking that was adequate – but no more – in conjunction with the single rear disc.

Although the spine frame design appeared dated in comparison with the latest alloy twin-beam constructions, the Trophy handled very well. In a straight line it was totally stable at all speeds, and barely gave a twitch even in bumpy high-speed curves. Chassis geometry was fairly conservative, and at 529lbs the bike was no lightweight. But the Triumph's steering was neutral, suspension was good and the bike could be hustled along a twisty road at a very respectable rate.

The Trophy's efficient full fairing, large fuel tank and comfortable seat were also well designed. Along with the Triumph's impressive strength and reliability, they combined to create a superb sports-

tourer that was competitive with long-standing Japanese favourites such as Kawasaki's ZZ-R1100 and Yamaha's FJ1200. If the Trophy had a fault, it was simply that its four-cylinder engine layout and conservative styling were unexceptional.

Few riders complained after they'd tried the Trophy 1200, which became a long-standing success for the British firm. In subsequent years it was refined with features including uprated brakes, a lower seat, improved finish and a clock in the dashboard. All helped to make the first new-generation Triumph an even more competent all-round superbike than ever.

'The bike could be hustled along a twisty road at a very respectable rate.'

SPECIFICATION: TRIUMPH TROPHY 1200	
ENGINE	Water-cooled DOHC 16-valve in-line four
DISPLACEMENT	1180cc
HORSEPOWER	125bhp @ 9000rpm
CARBURETTORS	4 x 36mm Mikuni
GEAR BOX	Five speed
FRAME	Tubular steel spine
WHEELBASE	58.7ins
WEIGHT	528lbs dry
TOP SPEED	153mph

Yamaha FJ1200

·····························

If the expression 'Superbike' sometimes encompasses ephemeral machines which fade as quickly out of the limelight as they flitted in, Yamaha's FJ1200 has proved to be one of the most enduring. A by-word for effortless long-distance work, it is comfortable, practical and fast. Very few bikes demolish miles quite so effortlessly. Until ousted by Triumph's 1200 Trophy (see page 82), it was the yardstick by which four-cylinder grunt was judged. Little wonder, then, that half the motorcycle press seem to have owned a FJ at one time or another.

Like good wine, the big Yamaha has improved progressively with the years. Initially launched in 1984 as the FJ1100, the machine was initially conceived as a sports bike, but soon came to be regarded as the definitive high-speed sports-tourer. In 1986, the engine was bored out from 1097 to 1188cc, adding to the air-cooled engine's already copious mid-range power. In '88 a 17in front wheel belatedly replaced the previous 16 incher, which both helped handling and reduced the front tyre's excessive wear. At the same time the brakes were uprated to four-piston calipers, and hydraulic anti-dive abandoned.

1991 saw the biggest redesign yet. ABS brakes were offered as an option (FJ1200A). A new, sturdier version of the original 'perimeter' frame with rubber-mounted engine replaced the previous chassis, in which the engine was solidly bolted as a stressed member. Throughout its long life the FJ has also received innumerable detail changes, notably to screen and seat, aimed at improving its long-distance capability. At one time a shaft-drive option, as fitted to Yamaha's equally venerable XJ900, was rumoured to be imminent. The 1200, however, steadfastly makes do with a chain.

The heart of the FJ is its engine. Although now dated in concept, it is supremely robust and works superbly on this class of bike – a real autobahn bruiser. Where many other Superbikes rocket to 160mph and well beyond, the FJ12 struggles to reach 150. Several sports 600s are as quick. Yet very few machines are this easy. Bottomless midrange power makes overtaking effortless, and the top gear take-up from 100mph can embarrass more powerful machines. Pre-'91 examples suffer from buzzy

vibration at certain revs; later, rubber-mounted models are silky-smooth throughout the range.

With this class of machine, stability and steering are far more important considerations than the ability to flick through chicanes like a Honda Fireblade. The FJ is a big, heavy bike, but carries its weight low. Handling is all-round competent, but marred by somewhat limited ground-clearance two-up. Fitted with the right tyres, it behaves well, but it is very tyre sensitive. Michelin radials seem to work best. The brakes are excellent on later models (the entire front end is the same as the FZR1000's), and the optional ABS anti-lock system is the best on the market.

Add an effective (but not over-large) fairing, a seat more than roomy enough for two, and the ability to lug huge amounts of luggage, and you begin to appreciate the FJ's real-world value. Perhaps its only serious flaw as the ultimate sports tourer is its limited tank range – at 37mpg, you can easily find yourself looking for petrol stations every 150 miles. But despite its age, the big FJ still represents a supremely practical package for the long-haul rider. It is not the quickest Superbike, and it is certainly not the sexiest, but year-in, year-out, it does what many do not: it really works.

'Very few bikes demolish miles quite so effortlessly.'

Compared to more recent superbikes, the FJ's handling is ponderous with a marked lack of ground clearance two-up. Comfort, though, is hard to beat.

SPECIFICATION:	**YAMAHA FJ1200**
ENGINE	Air-cooled DOHC 16-valve transverse four
DISPLACEMENT	1188cc
HORSEPOWER	125bhp @ 9000rpm
CARBURETTORS	4 x 36mm Mikuni CV
GEAR BOX	Five speed
FRAME	Square-section steel perimeter
WHEELBASE	58.9ins
WEIGHT	546lbs dry
TOP SPEED	146mph

Big air-cooled engine lacks the latest technology, but is a by-word for big-hearted power.

Yamaha YZF1000R Thunderace

....

'Thunderace is the Sensible Superbike.'

Subtle styling changes give the Thunderace a new look, notably at the front of its reshaped fairing. But the mighty YZF1000R has much in common with its FZR1000 predecessor — notably its ability to combine speed and fine handling with a reasonable degree of comfort.

Yamaha's aim with its YZF1000R Thunderace was simple: to build the best-performing superbike on the road. In designing a replacement for the long-successful FZR1000, the Japanese giant's intention was not to compete head-on with singleminded race-replicas such as Honda's Fireblade and Suzuki's GSX-R750, but to produce an ultra-powerful road rocket that could hold its own on the track too.

And that's exactly what the Thunderace is. Retaining the basic FZR1000 format of 20-valve, four-cylinder engine and twin-beam aluminium frame, the Thunderace features sharp styling, generous midrange power, superb handling and even a reasonable amount of comfort. By superbike standards it's almost an all-rounder – but that

versatility does not come at the expense of speed or sheer excitement.

Beneath the restyled bodywork, the Ace's watercooled, 1002cc motor is internally unchanged from its FZR predecessor apart from forged pistons – lighter and stronger than the previous cast variety – and a lighter crankshaft. A bank of 38mm downdraft Mikuni carbs helps boost midrange output on the way to an unchanged claimed peak of 145bhp at 10,000rpm.

The Thunderace's frame is borrowed not from the FZR1000 but from the YZF750. Its twin-spar aluminium construction is essentially similar, but the wheelbase is significantly shorter than the FZR's, aiding manoeuvrability. The frame holds a pair of conventional front forks of massive 48mm

diameter, and a single rear shock which, like the forks, is fully adjustable for damping.

The Ace's riding position is instantly familiar to anyone who's ridden a big FZR, and so is the engine's response to a handful of throttle. The revs rise with stunning speed towards the 11,000rpm redline as the Yamaha powers smoothly towards a top speed of around 170mph. Top-end performance is fearsome, but it's the Thunderace's storming midrange output that is much more useful on the road. The old FZR1000 was much-loved for its midrange grunt, and its successor has even more of the same thing.

The Ace's handling is equally impressive, managing to combine super-sports lightness and precision with a generous amount of stability. Despite its racy steering geometry and short wheelbase, the Thunderace doesn't quite have the razor-sharp steering feel of some sportsters – partly because, at 436lbs, it's slightly heavier.

But if the YZF loses out fractionally in its speed of steering, it's still a brilliantly agile, neutral-handling machine that would run rings round its FZR predecessor and most other bikes on the road. Suspension at both front and rear is excellent. And the Yamaha's front brakes, whose four-piston calipers have a one-piece construction instead of the normal bolted-together halves (increasing rigidity), are arguably the best in all motorcycling.

Other aspects of the Thunderace uphold the Yamaha tradition of building super-sports bikes that are tolerably comfortable over long distances. Its screen is too low for sustained high-speed use but gives reasonable protection. Switchgear and instrumentation are sensibly laid out, the fuel tank holds a reasonable 20 litres and the seat is broad – although a pillion has nothing solid to hold.

In many respects the YZF1000R Thunderace is the Sensible Superbike – if such a description could ever be used of a vehicle that accelerates from a

standstill to 150mph in about the time it takes to read this sentence. The Yamaha has neither the brute power of Honda's Super Blackbird nor the lightning reflexes of Suzuki's GSX-R750 – but in many situations it's faster than both. And the way the Thunderace combines its speed with all-round ability makes it a hugely impressive machine.

The Thunderace does not steer particularly quickly, but its high-speed stability is immense.

The Yamaha's front end is excellent, featuring hugely thick front forks and supremely powerful brakes.

SPECIFICATION: YAMAHA YZF1000R THUNDERACE	
ENGINE	Water-cooled DOHC 20-valve in-line four
DISPLACEMENT	1002cc
HORSEPOWER	145bhp @ 10,000rpm
CARBURETTORS	4 x 38mm Mikuni CV
GEAR BOX	Five speed
FRAME	Aluminium alloy beam
WHEELBASE	56.3ins
WEIGHT	436lbs dry
TOP SPEED	170mph

Yamaha GTS 1000

When it comes to bringing technological innovation to mass-produced motorcycles, Yamaha leads the way with its revolutionary GTS1000.

The GTS was the first mass-production superbike of the modern age to use a front suspension system that didn't employ a pair of telescopic forks and a chassis that doesn't run more or less in a straight line from the steering head to the swingarm pivot.

Motorcycle manufacturers have long searched for a method of suspending the front wheel of a motorcycle that doesn't rely on conventional telescopic forks. 'Teles' are unsatisfactory for several reasons – they are prone to flexing under braking and when cornering, and then cause the front end of the bike to 'dive' under braking. The search for a realistic alternative has been the Holy Grail of motorcycle engineering.

Yamaha's alternative front end, as featured on the GTS1000, is a single-sided front swingarm with hub-centre steering not unlike one front wheel of a car. Separating the steering function from the

Bold styling and high price of Yamaha's 'flagship' GTS has tempered sales, but expect to see more such technology on future models.

suspension should, in theory, produce a bike that steers, corners and brakes better than a bike with conventional forks.

The GTS's Omega chassis is different from that of a conventional bike because the front suspension removes the necessity for a headstock. The aluminium-alloy frame is a squat box-shaped affair which wraps around the engine, on to which are bolted the front and rear suspension systems, as well as the sub-frames necessary for the steering, seat and bodywork.

So how does this alternative front suspension system work? Basically it's in two parts. A single-sided swingarm attaches the front wheel to the chassis and a single shock-absorber bolts between the two. The steering is handled separately by a vertical cast aluminium-alloy spar that goes from the front axle to a steering box and thence to the handlebar crown.

The result is a bike that has one of the most sophisticated front suspension systems in production. The bad news is that, in the case of the GTS at least, this kind of suspension system offers no significant improvement over conventional telescopic forks. Being designed as a sports-touring

motorcycle the GTS is too long and carries too much weight to reap any benefits from hub-centre steering other than the elimination of front end dive under braking.

Indeed, the GTS is actually slower steering and more ponderous than many of its competitors, which surely isn't what Yamaha intended. Oddly enough, the harder the GTS is ridden the better it responds, which gives credence to claims that this is the way forward for sports bikes. It just doesn't seem to suit 550lb sports-tourers too well.

But what of the rest of the GTS? The engine is a state-of-the-art, 100bhp fuel-injected 1000cc in-line four with five valves per cylinder. The exhaust system features a three-way catalytic converter, and a tamper-proof ignition system. The front brake is also worthy of mention. The single-sided front swingarm means that only one disc brake can be fitted to the GTS, so Yamaha have equipped the GTS's single 320mm ventilated disc with a six-piston caliper for stupendous stopping power.

The GTS's performance is brisk rather than

exceptional, with a top-speed nudging 140mph. Although it shares the same basic layout as the Yamaha FZR1000, modifications to the valve timing and the fuel-injection system, ensure that the GTS only puts out 100bhp but with a substantial increase in mid-range power.

The GTS1000 is technologically very ambitious, and presents some interesting solutions to age-old problems. But ultimately it is an example of technology for technology's sake rather than a major step forward in motorcycle design.

Sure-footedness of the GTS's novel front suspension comes into its own on bumpy Lakeland back roads such as these.

'The result is a bike that has one of the most sophisticated front suspension systems in production.'

SPECIFICATION: YAMAHA GTS1000	
ENGINE	Liquid-cooled DOHC 20-valve in-line four
DISPLACEMENT	1002cc
HORSEPOWER	100bhp @ 9000rpm
CARBURETTORS	Electronic fuel injection
GEAR BOX	Five speed
FRAME	Aluminium-alloy Omega twin beam
WHEELBASE	58.8ins
WEIGHT	542lbs dry
TOP SPEED	140mph

Yamaha V-Max 1200

'Trying to go fast on a V-Max anywhere other than a straight line is not a relaxing experience!'

It's too big, too fat, too heavy, it won't stop and it doesn't handle. But – my! – is it *fast*.

By the mid-'eighties, motorcycle design had come a long way. From the early, over-powered and ill-handling Japanese superbikes, had evolved machines which took their cues from the racetrack and had tyres, suspension and steering to match. Suzuki's GSX-R750 and Yamaha's FZ750 typified the new breed.

But there will always be those who are less concerned with all-round performance than with sheer, brute power and the thrill of violent standing start acceleration. The Yamaha V-Max was designed just for them.

When it was first introduced in 1985, the V-Max caused a sensation, as much for its styling as its potential performance. The high-barred, low-slung look was based on the American cruiser style – bikes made for showing off in illegal sprints on impromptu drag strips on public roads. Real drag bikes had already evolved into long-wheelbased, front-heavy machines designed specifically for speed. Cruiser style puts the emphasis on *looking* fast – lots of noise and the ability to leave long strips of burnt rubber off the startline are more important than actual times.

And with a claimed 145bhp, the V-Max was capable of leaving a line of rubber all the way to the horizon – rear tyres on V-Maxes live short and tortured, but exciting lives.

The V-Max is completely dominated by its engine. At the time its V-four layout was a high-tech departure from the in-line fours that powered most Japanese motorcycles (only Honda built V-fours in any numbers). It featured a novel carburettor arrangement which meant each cyclinder was fed by two carburettors, then a gate moved to allow those same two carburettors to fill a different cylinder, thus eliminating the 'dead' time that usually occurs during a bike's combustion cycle. The result was midrange power that was literally like nothing any rider had experienced before, without sacrificing peak power. For a four cylinder engine it made its power at comparatively low revs – the red line was at just 8,500rpm. Visually, the massive black and silver V-four is the centrepiece of the bike's styling. And once on the move, the slightly lumpy power delivery – and the sheer amount of power it delivers – distract attention from the bike's handling.

It was the handling, more than the excess of power, that got the V-Max a reputation as a bike for would-be He-Men. It weaves, it wobbles, and it has so little ground clearance that a cornering V-Max strikes showers of sparks wherever it goes. The tyres are built for long life, not grip, and the brakes are only just about up to the job of hauling the V-Max's bulk down from speed. Trying to go fast on a V-Max anywhere other than a straight line is not a relaxing experience!

None of this matters to V-Max owners. Most don't even care that the top speed is 'only' 140mph. For a start, the lack of a fairing means hanging on at anything over 100mph is gruelling work. No, V-Max owners know that for that moment when the lights change to green (whether on the drag strip or the high street) what matters is how quickly and impressively the bike gets off the line.

In this, the V-Max is the motorcycling equivalent of the huge American muscle cars of the 'seventies – built for fun in a land where the speed limit is 55mph. It may not be the fastest or best-handling bike available, but it's become a modern classic for one reason – there is nothing else in Creation quite like a V-Max.

SPECIFICATION: YAMAHA V-MAX

ENGINE	Water-cooled DOHC 16-valve V-four
DISPLACEMENT	1198cc
HORSEPOWER	145bhp @ 8000rpm
CARBURETTORS	4 x 35mm Mikuni
GEAR BOX	Five speed
FRAME	Steel cradle
WHEELBASE	62.6ins
WEIGHT	578lbs dry
TOP SPEED	140mph

Whether it's a standard V-Max (right) or a special such as the Egli (below), only the devastating punch of the imposing V-four engine really matters. UK versions, sadly, have their power restricted.

Yamaha XJR1200

When Yamaha decided to enter the retro-bike market with a big, unfaired four-cylinder roadster, the perfect powerplant was already close to hand. The FJ1200 sports-tourer had been hugely popular for years due largely to its superbly tractable air cooled, 16-valve engine. This faithful brute of a motor was detuned, its cylinder fin-tips were polished, and it was put on display at the heart of a twin-shock musclebike called the XJR1200.

Yamaha lacked the four-stroke tradition of Kawasaki and Honda, whose Zephyr and CB1000 models the XJR was created to challenge. But the new bike's lines contained a hint of the 1978-model XS1100 four, and its all-black colour scheme echoed that of the later XS1100S Midnight Special. Maybe the lack of an illustrious predecessor was an advantage, because the clean, simply styled XJR was an undeniably good-looking machine.

FJ1200-based engine is the ideal candidate for a Retro musclebike. In XJR form, the air-cooled four puts out even more mid-range torque.

The 1188cc motor was placed in a new round-tube steel frame which, like the square-section FJ frame, incorporated a bolt-on lower rail to allow engine removal. Forks were conventional 43mm units, while at the back the XJR had a pair of remote-reservoir shocks from Öhlins, the Swedish suspension specialist firm owned by Yamaha. A pair of broad 17-inch wheels, the front holding big 320mm front discs with four-piston calipers, completed a purposeful profile.

From the rider's conveniently low seat the Yamaha gave a view of slightly raised handlebars, and chrome-rimmed instruments with a central fuel gauge. The engine contained numerous internal modifications to bring peak power output down to 97bhp at 8000rpm, from the FJ1200's 123bhp, and developed even more of the addictive low-rev torque for which the big four had long been renowned. Not that the motor hinted at the power waiting within, as it fired up with a mechanical rustle and a restrained burble from short twin silencers.

The upright riding position and that big, lazy engine set the tone of the bike, encouraging gentle riding and minimal use of the smooth-shifting five-speed gearbox. The XJR responded crisply from as low as 2000rpm in top gear, which made for effortless overtaking, and remained impressively smooth at almost all engine speeds. Acceleration was fearsome above 4000rpm, the handlebars tugging hard at the rider's shoulders as the Yamaha surged smoothly forward. If you hung on and kept the throttle open, it kept pulling remorselessly all the way to 140mph.

Handling was competent for this class of machine and the XJR remained stable at speed, despite the forces being fed into it by the human parachute at the handlebars. The Yamaha always felt like a fairly big, heavy bike, but it changed direction without a great deal of effort. Suspension at both ends was compliant enough for a comfortable ride, but firm enough to allow reasonably spirited cornering. Dunlop's fat radial tyres gave more than enough grip to exploit all the available ground-clearance, and the big front disc brakes were superbly powerful.

Japanese riders were the first to discover this first-hand, as the XJR was introduced as a home-market bike in 1994, before being released elsewhere a year later. Most of those who rode it were impressed. Inevitably, the XJR1200 shared the limitations of every big naked bike, in that the exposed riding position soon made using the engine's top-end performance tiring. But the big four's flexible power delivery made up for that. And the Yamaha's solid handling, handsome looks and general feel of quality made the XJR many riders' choice as the best big retro-bike of all.

SPECIFICATION: YAMAHA XJR1200	
ENGINE	Air-cooled DOHC 16-valve in-line four
DISPLACEMENT	1188cc
HORSEPOWER	97bhp @ 8000rpm
CARBURETTORS	4 x 37mm Mikuni
GEAR BOX	Five speed
FRAME	Tubular steel
WHEELBASE	58.5ins
WEIGHT	488lbs dry
TOP SPEED	140mph

Yamaha were late to clamber on board the Retro bandwagon, but the brutally handsome XJR1200 hits the spot.

Wide 'bars and upright riding position make the big Yamaha surprisingly agile through the turns, but this is still a massive machine to throw around.

Yamaha YZF750

....

Yamaha's FZ750 had been one of the company's best-sellers in the mid-'eighties, but by the early 'nineties it was dated – outhandled and outpowered by a new generation of alloy-framed, fat-tyred race replicas. Rumours of a replacement had been rife since Kawasaki launched the ZXR750 in 1989. But at that time Yamaha's answer was to launch the OW01, (a limited edition – and extremely expensive – World Superbike contender), and let the FZ soldier on as a road bike.

But by late 1992, the OW01 had also reached the end of its potential in world-class competition – now it was time to build a bike for the racetrack as well as the road.

The YZF750 was launched at the beginning of 1993 and quickly got a name for itself as a nimble, quick-steering sportster that handled more like a 600 than a big 750. It was based on the well-proven OW01 design, but developed to the point where no parts are interchangeable between the two.

Importantly for road riders, the YZF's road manners didn't need to be compromised by its track aspirations. A limited-edition SP version was built for racing, with a close-ratio gearbox, stiffer, multi-adjustable suspension, a single race seat and huge carburettors. That left the standard YZF with more useable gear ratios, proper pillion accommodation and far better engine behaviour than the SP. In fact, only the SP's adjustable suspension made YZF owners jealous. Yamaha listened to them and the standard YZF soon sprouted fully-adjustable Öhlins suspension front and rear.

The new suspension helped to make an already quick-steering and sweet-handling bike into a real road weapon. Surprisingly for a 750, it's easy to handle on twisty backroads, and civilised enough to cover long distances in reasonable comfort. That's partly down to the quality of the suspension, which allows relatively soft springs without compromising control – bumpy bends don't throw the YZF off line, or throw the rider out of his seat. But if you really want to experience the YZF's mind-expanding limits safely you need smooth, open roads or the freedom of a race track.

Because the YZF is fast. Not just in terms of outright speed – Kawasaki's ZXR is a little faster in still conditions. What makes the YZF's engine

Better looking and far, far cheaper than the Yamaha OW01 from which it is derived, the YZF is the classiest transverse four in the 750cc division.

Despite its superb credentials as a road bike, the YZF has never quite had the development to deliver in world superbike competition. The potential, though, is certainly there.

'The new suspension helped to make an already quick-steering and sweet-handling bike into a real road weapon.'

special is its smooth, linear midrange power delivery. For this, we have to thank Yamaha's unique EXUP system. The EXUP (it stands for Exhaust Ultimate Powervalve) is a valve in the exhaust collector pipe that opens and closes at pre-set revs, and fools the engine into thinking it has an exhaust pipe specifically tuned for those revs. The result is apparent as soon as you ride the YZF – where its competitors have little low-down pull, followed by peak power coming in with a bang, the YZF just pulls, and pulls, and pulls, from 3,000rpm all the way to the 13,000rpm redline.

Slowing the YZF down from its 160mph+ top speed are some of the most powerful front brakes fitted to any road bike. Twin discs are gripped so hard by six-piston calipers it's not unknown for the discs to warp under the strain. Other bikes now wear six-piston brakes (including some Triumphs and Suzukis), but the YZF was the first production bike to boast them as standard.

But its instant success as a road bike wasn't to be mirrored on the track. It was to be late 1994 before the YZF proved its worth and achieved its first serious international success – victory at the Bol d'Or 24-hour race in the hands of brothers and ex-GP racers Christian and Dominique Sarron. The race bike had finally caught up with the road bike.

SPECIFICATION: YAMAHA YZF750	
ENGINE	Water-cooled DOHC 20-valve in-line four
DISPLACEMENT	749cc
HORSEPOWER	122bhp @ 12,000rpm
CARBURETTORS	4 x 38mm Mikuni
GEAR BOX	Six speed
FRAME	Deltabox aluminium twin beam
WHEELBASE	55.9ins
WEIGHT	432lbs
TOP SPEED	160mph

YZF's 'Fox-eye' headlamps and superb six-piston front brakes set a trend. Its performance simply sets the pulse racing.

Index

ABS (anti-lock brakes) 17, 19, 84
Agostini, Giacomo 60

Bakker, Nico 8
    QCS1000 8-9
Bandit, Suzuki 68-69
Bimota
    Furano 10
    SB6R 12-13
    Tesi 1D 14-15
    YB11 Superleggera 10-11
Bing carburettors 18
Bloor, John 78, 82
BMW
    K1200RS 7, 16-17
    R1100RS 18-19
Boxer engines 18
Brando, Marlon 80
Brembo brakes 10, 24, 29, 61
Buell, Erik 20
    S1 Lightning 20-21

Cagiva, Elefant 22-23
Carillo con-rods 30
Centauro, Moto Guzzi 62-63
Cosworth pistons 30
Cruise control, 45

Daytona 62, 64
    Triumph 74, 76
Dell'Orto carburettors 65
Desmodromic valvegear 22, 27, 28
Ducati
    and Cagiva Elefant 22-23
    888, and 916 26
    900 Monster 24-25
    900SS engine 24, 28
    916 26-27, 51
    900 Superlight 28-29

Egli, Fritz 30
    Harley-Davidson 30-31
'Evolution', Harley engines 30, 32, 36
EXUP, exhaust system 95

Ferrari, Virginio 10
Ferraris, versus Kawasaki, 58
Fireblade, Honda 42-43
FireStorm, Honda 46-47
Fogarty, Carl 26
Forcelle Italia suspension 61

Gold Wing, Honda 44-45

Hailwood, Mike 60

Harley-Davidson
    and Buell 20
    and Egli 30
    Dyna Glide 32-33
    Electra Glide 34-35
    Heritage Softail 36-37
    XL1200S Sportster Sport 38-39
Hinckley, Triumph factory 74, 78, 80, 82
Honda
    CBR900RR Fireblade 42-43
    and Kawasaki ZX-9R 54
    and Suzuki RF900 70
    CBR1100XX Super Blackbird 48-49,
    87
    and Kawasaki ZZ-R1100 48
    F6C Valkyrie 40-41
    GL1500 Gold Wing 40, 44-45
    and Harley 35
    'RC30' VFR750R 50
    'RC45' RVF750R 50-51
    and Ducati 916 26
    VTR1000F FireStorm 46-47

Kawasaki
    1100 Zephyr 52-53
    Z1, Z1000 52
    ZX-7R 56-57
    ZX-9R 54-55, 70
    ZXR750 51, 56
    ZZ-R1100 58-59
    and Honda Fireblade 43
    and Triumph 83
Kayaba suspension 83
Keihin carburettors 46

Le Mans, Moto Guzzi 60
Lotus Engineering 74

Magni, Arturo 60
    Australia 60-61
Manley valves 30
Marconi, Pierluigi 13
Marzocchi suspension 22
Meriden, former Triumph factory 74, 82
Mikuni carburettors 11, 13, 28, 30, 86
Mikuni-Denso fuel-injection 72
Milwaukee, Harley factory 20, 32, 36
Moto Guzzi
    1100 Sport Injection 64-65
    Centauro 62-63

Ninja, Kawasaki 54
Nissin brakes 22, 46, 72, 75, 76, 83

Öhlins suspension 12, 22, 92, 94

Omega chassis system 88

Paris-Dakar rally 22
Performance Machine 21

Retro, style of motorcycle 52, 68, 81, 92
'Retro-tech', and Harleys 36

Schwantz, Kevin 66
'Screaming Eagle' tuning parts 20, 33
Sfida, Moto Guzzi 60
Showa suspension 28, 38, 75
Softail suspension 36
Speed Triple, Triumph 76-77
Sturgis, Harley-Davidson 32
Superbike world championship 26, 28, 94
Super Blackbird, Honda 48-49
Surtees, John 60
Suzuki
    GSF1200 Bandit 68-69
    GSX-R750 66-67
    GSX-R1100 12
    RF900 70-71
    TL1000S 72-73

Telelever suspension 16, 18
Thunderace, Yamaha 86-87
Tokico brake calipers 57
Triumph
    Sprint 78-79
    T509 Speed Triple 76-77
    T595 Daytona 74-75
    Thunderbird 80-81
    Trophy 82-83

'Uniplanar' frames 21

Valkyrie, Honda 40-41

Weber-Marelli fuel injection 63
White Power suspension 30, 61
Works Performance suspension 21

Yamaha
    FJ1200 84-85
    and Triumph Trophy 83
    and XJR1200 92
    GTS1000 88-89
    and BMW suspension 18
    OW01 94
    V-Max 90-91
    XJR1200 92-93
    YZF750 94-95
    YZF1000R Thunderace 10, 86-87